C0-AKQ-258

Exploring Canadian Values
Foundations for Well-Being

Suzanne Peters

CPRN Study No. F-01

ISBN 1-896703-02-X
© Canadian Policy Research Networks Inc., 1995

Available from
Renouf Publishing Co. Ltd.
1294 Algoma Road
Ottawa, On K1B 3W8
Tel.: (613) 741-4333   745-2665
Fax: (613) 741-5439

The findings of this Paper are the sole responsibility of the author and, as such, have not been endorsed by the individuals and agencies mentioned in the Appendices.

Contents

Foreword   *v*

1. ***Introduction and Overview***   **1**
   Identifying Canadians' Values – The Methodology   2
   Core Canadian Values   5
   Collective Responsibility and Individual Self-Reliance   6
   Balancing the "Welfare State" and the Need for Fiscal Restraint   7
   Changing Family Realities   14
   Working Through Conflicts and Trade-Offs   18

2. ***Canadians' Value Statements: Social Assistance Programs***   **21**
   Self-Reliance   21
   What Are the State's Responsibilities?   22
   Abuse of the Social Security System   23
   Encouraging Personal Autonomy   23
   Single Mothers Receiving Social Assistance   27
   Getting Out of the System   30

3. ***Canadians' Value Statements: Broad Social Programs***   **33**
   Health Care   34
   User Fees   34
   Education   38
   Other Programs   39

4. ***Canadians' Vision for Canada***   **43**
   Should the Majority Rule?   43
   Regional Equity   44
   Immigration   45
   Diversity and Equity   46

5.   *The View of Partnerships*   51
       Charitable Sector Partnerships   51
       Private Sector Partnerships   53

6.   *Government and Engagement*   55
       Waste and Inefficiency   55
       Trust in Government   58
       Democratic Engagement   59

Epilogue: Next Steps   65

Appendices
A   *Public Opinion Poll Databases*   71
B   *Discussion Group Methodology*   73
C   *Funders and Advisors*   77

Tables   79

Foreword

The scope for the public to participate in policy choices has eroded in recent times for many reasons. Experts dominate the debate because the issues are often technically complex; the power of decision is concentrated in government and corporate boardrooms; there are many conflicting voices seeking to influence decisions; the public policy agenda is overcrowded; the speed of change makes it hard to keep track; and so on.

Citizens are aware of this loss of participation. It makes them angry and frustrated. That anger is reported regularly in opinion polls. Governments are inefficient and wasteful, say the polls. But the polls also show that Canadians expect a great deal of their governments – they are angry but they have not given up. What is missing, at this stage in our history, is an opportunity for citizens to engage the issues in a thoughtful way and a means to transmit their conclusions to decision makers. This document represents the first stage of an effort to pilot in Canada pioneering techniques used in the United States to try to fill the void between the public and the policy-making process.

Daniel Yankelovich, in his book, *Coming to Public Judgment: Making Democracy Work in a Complex World* makes a distinction between the "top of mind" answers that the public give to pollsters, and the considered judgments that occur after citizens have worked through the issues with others. Yankelovich defines public judgment as a form of public opinion, which exhibits:

> "(1) more thoughtfulness, more weighing of alternatives, more genuine engagement with the issue, more taking into account a wide variety of factors than ordinary public opinion . . . and (2) more emphasis on the normative, valuing, ethical side of questions than on the factual, informational side." (p. 5)

To test the way in which these ideas might be applied in Canada, Suzanne Peters, Director of the Family Network of CPRN, designed a project that explores the values that Canadians uphold with respect to health, education, and social supports – the three main components of the social safety net. She began with a rich array of public opinion data for the past 15 years, using 18 different databases, including approximately 50 different polls. She then organized 25 extended discussion groups in eight cities, so that Canadians could talk to each other about their values, the changes they would like to see in social policy, and the principles that they believe should guide those changes. (Over half of these groups included randomly selected participants, the rest were composed of Family Service recipients.) Suzanne Peters has synthesized the two sources of data in this CPRN study. In addition, a brief summary of the findings has been published under the title *Exploring Canadian Values*.

The study is an arresting declaration of deeply felt views of Canadians. There is a remarkable appetite for change in programs. The values that surfaced have not changed dramatically over time, but the way in which Canadians see those values being expressed in programs and policies has changed quite considerably. There has been an evolution in their thinking about universality, for example, and their strong sense of collective responsibility is now balanced by recognition that families and individuals must take more responsibility for themselves and their kin. Despite the anger and frustration, there is still a deep sense of compassion in Canadians. There is also a deeply felt desire to participate in the public policy process.

Neither we nor the participants want the process to end here. Accordingly, we have begun to organize partnerships with organizations across the country that create a natural setting for this kind of dialogue – places of work, worship, recreation, and community action. These partners, with some initial help from CPRN, plan to organize discussion groups in the first half of 1996, which will involve many more Canadians in the process of "working through" from opinion to judgment on a range of issues that have much to do with who we are as a people.

I would like to thank Suzanne Peters for her energy and imagination in making the project happen, as well as the Advisory Committee, which included funders, experts, and frontline service providers – all are listed in Appendices B and C . I would also like to offer a special word of thanks to the Family Service Agencies who organized discussions groups and to the public opinion polling firms who gave us access to their data (listed in Appendix A). To our funders, who made the project possible, heartfelt thanks for their willingness to fund this pioneering work.

We hope the process will continue, and we look forward to the response of Canadians to the next round. After that, it will be up to policymakers to listen to what citizens are saying.

Judith Maxwell
President

Exploring Canadian Values
Foundations for Well-Being

Suzanne Peters

Suzanne Peters is Director of the Family Network, Canadian Policy Research Networks. Over the last 15 years, she has established a strong track record in the social policy field as a commentator and speaker, consultant, public servant, academic, and most recently, as Executive Director of a non-profit institute, The Policy Research Centre for Children, Youth and Families. Currently, as President of the Policy Research Group, Dr. Peters focuses on social justice, health and the well-being of families, children, women and vulnerable persons. She completed postdoctoral studies at the Université de Montréal, received a Ph.D. in sociology at McGill University, and also studied at Carleton University. Dr. Peters currently volunteers as a member of the Board of Canadian Outward Bound Wilderness School and the Family Service Agency of Metropolitan Toronto.

1. *Introduction and Overview*

The urgency of articulating the core commitments of Canadians – what we hold dear, what trade-offs and sacrifices we are willing to make, and what we see as the optimal level of well-being that can be achieved – has never been greater. With the reshaping of our social programs in a climate of fiscal restraint, and the uncertainties generated by the narrow margin in the October 30, 1995 Quebec referendum, Canadians have entered debates that will reshape our sense of ourselves and our nation.

One challenge before all of us – politicians, the corporate sector, media, policymakers, researchers, community leaders and the public – is to understand the foundations on which we can build a new social contract. Recognition and acknowledgement of shared values are critical to Canadians' sense of belonging and our ability to move forward. An equal challenge is to involve Canadians in the debates that define those common values and the processes that set out the country's social and economic objectives.

The first objective of this report is to explore the core values and principles Canadians want to use to define the scope and structure of our social safety net. The second objective is to examine the emerging state of public judgment, including the confusions and ambiguities that surface as we grapple with the contradictions and tensions of changing global and domestic forces.

In designing a new social contract in these difficult times, Canadians feel anger, loss, ambivalence, and uncertainty. We do not want to retreat on the social policy front. We want to retain the social capital of this country, enhance social cohesion, and strengthen the social fabric. At the same time, we want to exercise hard-headedness on the fiscal side. We accept the need for cuts in principle, but we do not want to lose cherished social programs. We see individual effort as ideal and necessary, but we accept collective responsibility when that effort fails or is impeded. We are angry about the lack of effectiveness and efficiency in government, but we see an important continuing role for governments in defining and implementing a new social contract.

Faced with these contradictions, Canadians are eager to begin to work through complexities, resolve conflicts, and secure a solid foundation for a fair, prosperous and caring society. This study, therefore, proposes a structure and process to involve Canadians in the debate in a way that ensures that their values are respected and reflected in decisions on social policy.

To discern Canadians' core values, this study examines a time-series of public opinion data drawn from 18 public opinion databases, comprised of approximately 50 polls between 1979 and 1995. These examine data on social, educational, economic and health issues. To understand values more deeply, this report also examines the results of 25 discussion groups with randomly recruited Canadians and with Canadians who were using social service agencies. These discussion groups were held in June and July of 1995.

This chapter of the report analyzes the overarching themes that arose in the examinations of poll data on values and the results of the discussion groups. Chapters two to six present compilations and analyses of the two information sources as they related to a number of key subjects. Chapters two and three present our analyses of Canadians' value statements on, respectively, social assistance and other social programs. Chapter four looks at critical background issues affecting Canadians' vision for their country. Chapter five deals with values related to the formation of partnerships for social goals, and chapter six presents Canadians' perceptions of governance and democratic engagement. The epilogue presents plans by the Canadian Policy Research Networks for further consultations with Canadians to advance the process of democratic engagement. The Appendices present our advisory process, funders, and the research methodology in greater detail.

Identifying Canadians' Values – The Methodology

The two data sources analyzed in this report, public opinion polls and discussion group findings, provide a strong counterpoint to each other. While public opinion data is often criticized as superficial, it offers the only continuing record of the values and commitments that Canadians have espoused in changing social, economic, and political times. Discussion group findings, on the other hand, offer rich and highly textured perspectives on Canadians' values.

Tracking public values – Poll data

The examination of public opinion poll data explores diverse issues and a breadth of information on values that has not been addressed together before. Comparisons of polling data over years have limits, however, including the fact that they must be considered as time-series rather than longitudinal data. Also, since even very similar questions asked in different polls may elicit different answers – both because of the sequence of the questions and the context of related questions – polls do not tell a precise story. The most reliable data here is based on the answers to identical questions asked in repeated polls.

Overall, the data give a broad-brush picture of Canadian values and demonstrate that, through changing times and shifting government priorities, Canadians' values in social policy are remarkably stable.

Identifying ambiguities and uncertainties – The discussion group process

This study simulated a process of public judgment, as described by Daniel Yankelovich, in his book *Coming to Public Judgment: Making Democracy Work in a Complex World*. The focus group exercises were designed to identify deeper values, as well as areas of uncertainty in public views on social policy. This process was purposively different from that of garnering public views through opinion polling or through conventional focus group techniques. In the public judgment process, the group leader explicitly allowed room for members to listen to one another, consider their internal value conflicts, and reflect on priorities. Rather than offering instant reactions, or arguing from set positions, participants were encouraged to tolerate ambiguity before coming to public judgment. In this way, members could develop a more informed and thoughtful view of the issues at hand.

In the present study, 25 groups of Canadians in eight cities participated in a series of exercises stimulating discussions of core values with respect to social programs. These discussions were placed squarely in the context of fiscal cuts.

In the first set of exercises, participants considered slightly conflicting value statements related to issues of governance, responsibility and equity. These statements are illustrated in the box below.

Conflicting Value Statements

Group One:
Governance, Individual Participation, Public Accountability

"Those elected to government soon lose touch with what people really want."

"If I don't do my bit in telling government what I want, how can I expect decisions that I like?"

"People like me don't have any say about what government does."

"I have as much control over the decisions that affect me as I want."

Group Two:
Individual Responsibility vs. Collective Responsibility

"We have a responsibility to take care of each other."

"Life is what you make it; if you sit back and do nothing you can't expect life to be good."

" People should not blame society for their problems because they're responsible for the choices they make."

"Society has a responsibility to take care of those who can't take care of themselves."

Group Three:
Fairness and Accessibility, Universality and Entitlement

"In a democracy the majority rules. The minority will have to fit in with the majority."

"Every Canadian deserves to have a minimum standard of living."

"It's more important for everyone to get the same thing rather than some groups getting special attention."

Acting as a panel of citizens, the second exercise asked participants to advise government about changes in Canada's social safety net; all groups had to resolve a series of complex trade-offs in public spending, either by cutting one of two programs or by funding one of two alternatives. These trade-offs forced participants to think through fundamental decisions as they wrestled with the kinds of cuts that could take place as social policy choices are made. The initial program trade-offs presented to participants are listed in the box below.

Program Trade-Offs

Care for babies

Fund a well-baby clinic program that provides free immunization and checkups to every child in the province.

Or provide intensive, individualized care and stimulation for babies with special problems, who would then be likely to have normal outcomes.

School lunches

Provide money to foster a partnership between charitable organizations and big business that could fund school lunch programs in needy areas.

Or fund a more limited program guaranteed to reach a smaller number of the most needy children.

Social assistance for teenagers

Allow applications for social assistance from individuals over the age of fourteen with stringent eligibility criteria.

Or increase the eligible age for receiving social assistance to 18.

Social assistance priorities

Reduce social assistance levels for sole support parents, mostly mothers with young children.

Or cut back on job training for 'willing and able to work' adults on social assistance.

Preventing or treating heart disease

Cut funds for break-through research on new preventative measures for heart disease.

Or cancel plans for a needed expansion of heart disease treatment clinics around the province.

Regional or central cancer clinic

Fund a state-of-the-art cancer clinic, including service in many languages, in the province's largest city.

Or fund basic cancer clinics with limited treatment facilities in at least six centres across the province.

Life prospects

Fund a cooperative university-employer program for new graduates, to facilitate their entry into the labour market.

Or fund a highly specialized treatment regime for cancer patients who have about a 30% chance of surviving past five years.

Given the differences between the two types of data examined in this study, one might expect the findings from one to dramatically differ from the other. Instead, this project has found a strong degree of concordance between the public opinion polls and the group discussions on many important issues. While the discussions refine and offer a rich texture to explain poll findings, they seldom directly contradict them.

When engaged in more complex considerations through the public judgment process, Canadian responses appear to be highly nuanced. As discussion ensues, participants modify positions in ways that reflect their underlying sense of compassion for others and their hopes that the values that underpin our current social safety net will not be abandoned.

In forming public judgment, participants often seek to define third and alternative options that reflect a new kind of balance between economic and social objectives. They work through options that call for a strategic reorientation of systems and structures.

While participants face difficult trade-offs and confront their differences directly, the vast majority find the process rewarding. They leave the discussion less angry and less anxious. Participants see this as a different kind of exercise than any in which they had previously engaged. They describe it a rare opportunity to deal reflectively with complex issues. Many promise to continue to talk about these issues with friends and family. Almost all participants request follow-up information on the project, and many volunteer to be further involved in activities related to this or other projects dealing with the values of Canadians.

While supporting opinion poll data, the discussion group findings shed a different light on public values than what might be assumed as a result of shifts in the electoral process. When voting, Canadians choose from set options drawn from the current political spectrum. In the public judgment process, they are offered an opportunity to redefine those options. In offering a "grey zone" for discussion that avoids the confines of polarized political and ideological debates, the public judgment process elicited opinions that contrast with the results of recent Canadian elections. These findings and others are discussed more fully below.

Core Canadian Values

While Canadians across regions, incomes, age groups, and education levels continue to work through their priorities, they share many common values. Almost all discussion group participants espoused the values of:

- self-reliance
- compassion leading to collective responsibility
- investment, especially in children as the future generation

- democracy
- freedom
- equality

- fiscal responsibility.

These values are deeply held and form a solid and stable foundation for public debate. Most of them are unchanged from those that shaped the original construction of our safety net.

What has changed is Canadians' certainty that we have designed the appropriate system to achieve these goals. This study confirms that Canadians are disillusioned with government. They have become sceptical about the piecemeal solutions offered by government responses. Concerned with achieving greater effectiveness and efficiency in programs, Canadians want systemic solutions. They want to do more than merely allay individual symptoms through fragmented approaches; they want to promote our collective well-being and find a cure for Canada's social and economic ills. Canadians also make it clear that they want fuller partnerships across sectors and to be more involved in the process of social policy restructuring.

In discussion groups, as participants simulated citizens' panels advising government, the current of ambivalence and scepticism became apparent. Participants' ambivalence came out initially in the ways in which they ranked the things they 'most value' and 'most want to change' about Canada. The most valued elements include our democracy and freedom, as well as aspects of social programs, particularly health care. The thing participants most wanted to change is the current level of government expenditure.

Differences in groups also emerged that required further investigation. Recipients of services tended to be somewhat more protective of the social safety net. Participants in randomly recruited groups tended to be somewhat more willing to cut. Since, these two groups also differed demographically, particularly in that service recipients were younger, the following analysis also explores whether polling data demonstrate significant differences by age of respondent. As we will see below, while core values are similar, younger Canadians in general tend to feel more threatened by the potential loss of social programs. Other differences in how the safety net is perceived were also explored in the polling data, including regional differences. It is important to underline that these differences are questions of degree rather than polarizations in the population. Canadians hold common values as expressed above; different groups of Canadians by age and region sometimes place a different weight on particular values.

Collective Responsibility and Individual Self-Reliance

Close to twice as many Canadians believe that, ideally, Canadian society should be "a unified body pursuing a common goal" as believe it should be "a collection of people independently pursuing their own goals" (Table 1). In achieving a common goal, Canadians in the 1990s expect government to play a critical role, but they want that role to be balanced with individual effort and self-reliance. Canadians' struggle to achieve this balance between collective responsibility and individual self-reliance is integral to the process of working through values and identifying principles to guide decisions about social policies and programs.

While Canadians strive to be self-reliant and think that individuals must take on more responsibility themselves, they recognize

"This last discussion uncovers a values conflict for me, because I feel on the one hand that we collectively, as the government, should

that circumstances are not always within an individual's direct control and so continue to see a collective role for government in providing a safety net. In 1993, 64% agreed that people are responsible for their own lives, but even more (84%) felt government has a responsibility to ensure that all citizens have the basic necessities of life, regardless of circumstances (Table 2). Those who have received welfare or social assistance, and those living in the Atlantic provinces, were least likely to see people as individually responsible.

In group discussions, participants amplified their views of self-reliance considerably. Individual effort and responsibility for one's actions was a strong value among all participants. Some participants told personal stories of sacrifices they made to avoid depending or continuing to depend on government assistance. Sometimes this meant separating families and spending little time parenting children.

Self-reliance was also often linked to images of democracy and freedom. Those who took responsibility for themselves were considered to have earned their democratic rights. By the same token, those who did not take responsibility were sometimes seen as abusing democratic privileges.

Collective responsibility reflects the democratic contract and an ecological view of providing for others as a means to strengthen links across the chain of societal well-being.

provide a safety net. On the other hand, I strongly agree with the people who have said that the individual and the family and the community should be trying to do things, but that government should still be there if all of that fails and those people fall through. Both are true..."

"In a democracy where we participate, I think the first premise that we have to make is that we're all responsible for the other guy."

"Because if we don't, there's a breakdown in taking care of people. If there's a breakdown somewhere along the line, the repercussions become massive."

"We have a responsibility as human beings in this country to take care of ourselves, to be educated, to be aware, and to contribute."

"I think that one of the reasons Canada is good and that life here is better than in lots of other countries of the world is that we try to take care of the people who have suffered misfortunes or who have fallen on bad times. I value that. If I didn't have a job or I was disabled in some horrible car accident and didn't have the right insurance, I would hope that I wouldn't be destitute on the street. In the meantime, being in health and in work, I expect to do that for other people."

"The country is only as healthy as the poor in the country."

Canadians hold highly complex views of the total social fabric, and they are cautious about the consequences of rending part of it without doing damage to the whole.

Balancing the "Welfare State" and the Need for Fiscal Restraint

Canadians have become deeply attached to the welfare state that emerged after the war and reached its full development during the 1970s. In fact, until recently, social policy and programs enjoyed a kind of benevolent neglect and discussions about them fuelled little controversy. Health care, social services and education ranked consistently low as public priorities in opinion polls until 1993, but have since come to share the spotlight with the economy and unemployment. This change in poll results, which was mirrored in the results of group discussions, suggests that social and health programs became priorities only when they could no longer be taken for granted (Table 3).

Canadians confront the implications of the fiscal realities of the 1990s only with reluctance. Not surprisingly, they are having a difficult time letting go. The findings here suggest that Canadians are not willing to beat a chaotic retreat on the social policy front.

Polling data demonstrate that most Canadians view many social programs as vital and are uncomfortable with the idea of reducing spending on them. Programs such as health care, education, Unemployment Insurance, and Old Age Security are viewed as entitlements. The necessity of fiscal restraint is widely accepted, however. So, while Canadians are deeply concerned with the current level of government expenditure and with improving government efficiency and accountability, they want government to respond compassionately on social policy issues.

Canadians predict that what are seen as inevitable program cuts will have negative impacts and do not want to relinquish the foundations of well-being offered by social, health, and education programs. A Spring 1993 poll showed that a majority of Canadians imagine either more limited coverage or the disappearance of medicare in coming years, and most of

"We are Canadians and we take care of each other."

"We are all milliseconds away from being in that situation ourselves, and that's what we have to remember as we battle through this thing. The poor is the wrong target."

them see this as a 'bad thing' (Table 4). They want to temper any cuts with a sense of collective responsibility tied to their national identity. Three in four Canadians are personally very concerned about the future of social programs and are worried that people who really need programs could be hurt (Table 5). A paramount value is to ensure that the truly needy do not suffer as Canadians get their fiscal house in order.

While Canadians are slowly beginning to see some programs as more essential than others, making these choices is not easy and evokes regret and ambivalence. In 1991, a large proportion (74%) said they would be upset by a freeze in provincial and health payments (Table 6). By 1993, a bare majority (54%) said that they would accept cuts in services in exchange for greater control over the deficit. While 34% were prepared to maintain programs even if that meant a deficit, 12% did not know (Table 7). While in theory willing to forego some services, in practice Canadians are reluctant to sacrifice actual programs. In 1992, most still said they would rather raise taxes or increase the deficit than accept a wide range of cuts, income supports such as children's benefits and income supports for the unemployable (Table 8). The exceptions were doctors, services and income support for unemployed Canadians, which most appear to be prepared to cut.

In forming public judgment, many discussion group participants also refined their initial positions to seek options that reflected a balance between economic and social objec-

"Unemployment triggers sickness and leads people to rely on social assistance. It is a domino."

tives. They saw this balance as key to the kind of society they live in. They are striving to renew a spirit of positive purpose, regain a sense of control, and discover how to foster social cohesion as the basis for creating a more civil society. The sophistication and complexity of Canadians' perspectives make it clear that they see changes in social policy as integrally related to objectives in economic policy and vice versa. Thus offering adequate social programs is seen as a route to ensuring that Canadians are able to work, and getting people back to work is seen as essential to reinvesting in social programs. This leads Canadians to reflect deeply on the other ways to reduce costs. Despite the fact that the trade-offs for this study were focused on social programs, some group participants wanted to put other kinds of program cuts in the equation. These were likely to include perceived waste by government and lost tax revenues from the corporate sector, but sometimes also potential cuts to defense and subsidies to business.

"We're not just dealing with a return on our investment. We're talking about students, we're talking about the mental well-being of our young citizens and our future population. It is a health issue: a good morale affects the health of our nation."

"Employment is the driver in this country; we have to think of ways to improve the workforce. It's in creating wealth that we have money to do cancer research."

"The more people in society who are working, the more taxes we're going to have and sooner or later we're going to be able to pay for both programs."

"Because if you get everybody working, it would be a healthier country ... What I meant by healthy too is not only your health, your country's health. Instead of taking from the government, you're putting back into it."

Sharing the benefits of productivity or providing "last resort" help?

Canadians' desire to preserve social programs, while at the same time to reduce government spending, is situated in a complex interplay of changing global and domestic forces: global competition and new technology, media coverage, changing demographics, shifting political agendas and allegiances, and a diminishing role for and fading confidence in governments.

The process of working through necessary change evokes a fundamental rethinking of the role of social programs. Where social spending was once almost unanimously envisioned as a mechanism to achieve positive public good, it is increasingly seen as the means to avoid the negative repercussions of inevitable global forces. Rather than comparing Canada to the best-case scenarios of societies that retain relatively high levels of social services, many Canadians have started to draw worse

"... with the slow dismantling happening because of the hot political issues right now – welfare, for example, and all these programs being targeted – universality is going to disappear. We are going to become more like the States where it's the 'haves' and the 'have-nots' and the gap is going to get wider and wider. The repercussions will also be a higher crime rate and the whole shemozzle, and that's the sad part."

case comparisons, most often to the United States. Many have started to adopt minimalist expectations

9

– testing ideas for policies and programs against the litmus strip of whether or not they will help Canadians to avoid the social and economic ills plaguing our neighbours to the south.

Increasingly, Canadians tend to see the cup as half empty rather than half full. Today's troubled economy and two successive recessions have led many Canadians to raise questions about the affordability and appropriateness of our social safety net. In the climate of economic prosperity of the 1960s and 1970s, most Canadians came to see social spending as an opportunity to equalize the benefits of productivity to all citizens. Today many harken back to the 1940s' view of social programs as remedial measures for an unfortunate few. Given fiscal realities, many Canadians are returning to a view of the social safety net as a last resort.

Despite this context, most Canadians do not see our economic difficulties as a reason to delay social program reform. In 1994, 72% agreed that now is as good a time as any, while only 25% felt that the time is not right given high unemployment. Regional and education differences were apparent, however, with more vulnerable Canadians wanting to exercise more caution, including those living in the Atlantic provinces, as well as those with only some high school education (Table 9).

The desire for reform does not mean that Canadians are willing to relinquish social programs: 1994 attitudes suggest that social programs give Canadians a sense of security and generate worries that people who need them will be hurt by cuts, especially among younger and Atlantic Canadians (Table 10). A majority see programs as helping people in time of need, but an even larger proportion see the need for reform of social programs (Table 11). A large proportion are concerned that existing programs make it too easy for people to give up looking for work (Table 10). A majority of Canadians, 7 in 10, see social programs as essential to Canadian identity (Table 11).

Similarly, discussion groups, in constructing a third option to the trade-off between cuts in welfare or cuts in training, consistently devised programs that they felt would offer greater incentives for labour force participation and help recipients make the transition back to work. These complex contradictions suggest that governments and the public must come to terms with massive pressures for change in designing programs that will offer needed incentives without abandoning the needs of those in crisis. Considering core values will provide a foundation for Canadian identity through a new social contract; defining common principles will offer parameters for policies and programs.

What is government's role?

Unlike harsher views in favour of fiscal restraint that may "blame the victim" for his or her own poverty, Canadians do not feel that the unsuccessful "have only themselves to blame." Fewer than one in five take the position that the poor are poor because they do not try hard enough; only one in five agree that "the wealthy and powerful keep them poor" (Table 12). Canadians are apparently willing to acknowledge that other, more systemic factors lie at the root of poverty. Belief in government's ability to eradicate poverty is low, however: three in four respondents agreed that "no matter what society and governments do, there will always be poor people in Canada" (Table 13).

While one in four Canadians agreed that "government programs and policies can do little to solve the difficulties children face," one in three disagreed (Table 14). Clearly the wish and vision of personal responsibility is keenly felt by many Canadians, but it goes hand-in-glove with a sense of compassion for those who cannot help themselves and a belief that governments have a role to play.

Economic conditions clearly drive perceptions of the role of government, particularly in the area of income security. During the 1980s boom, there was less support for the idea of government ensuring a job and a decent standard of living than during the more economically troublesome 1990s.

In 1987, 5 in 10 Canadians believed that government had a responsibility to "see to it that everyone has a job and a decent standard of living," and a similar number agreed that they are "glad that I have a government that looks after me in so many ways" (Table 15). Over 8 in 10 agreed in 1989 that government has a responsibility to ensure that all Canadians have the basic necessities of life (Table 16).

"All these social programs are valid. Give us something that we really don't want and make it an easy choice."

"You can't cut one or the other. You just can't."

"I think to guide them on how to make decisions about health reform, education and social reform, they need to look at everything. It's like a deck of cards. If you move one card, the entire thing falls apart. So that what they need to do is step back and take a look at how one decision will affect everything."

By 1993, over 6 in 10 Canadians voiced support for governments' role in ensuring that everyone has a job and a decent standard of living. While more than two-thirds of the general public believed that 'government must do more to reduce the income gap between rich and poor Canadians', those with less education were even more likely to agree (Table 17). Over 8 in 10 agreed that government has a responsibility for the poor and the elderly (Table 18).

Despite public rhetoric about the developed dependency of welfare programs, not all Canadians blame programs for making people more dependent. Programs to help children in low-income families were seen as "making more people dependent" by almost 4 in 10 of the general public, but an equal number were neutral and almost 1 in 4 disagreed (Table 15).

In 1994, almost 7 in 10 Canadians believed that the federal government had a role to play to "redistribute wealth in order to maintain social equality" (Table 19). Income levels and employment status, often tied to generational opportunities, appear to be key to understanding different views of the appropriate role of government.

Differences between elites and general public opinion

Questions surround the potential division of public and elite opinion on a number of priorities. Data on different elite groups appears to tell different stories. Recent data from an upper-class defined elite sampled by EKOS suggests a sharp divide between the general public and this elite. This elite group generally see a more minimalist role for government across the board. In 1994, just over 4 in 10 members of this elite, compared to almost 7 in 10 members of the general public saw a role for government in redistributing wealth (Table 19), as well as different roles across the board.

In contrast, a high elite group interviewed in-depth on public sector issues in 1994 through the Opinion Leader Research Program (OLRP) appears to agree with the general public on a wide range of issues articulated in this study. In particular, the higher elite group sees the need for a continuing role for government in defining the social dimensions of Canada; like ordinary Canadians, they want better government, but not necessarily less government.

Data related to the elite sample, as cited numerically below, refer to the EKOS survey rather than the OLRP, which is largely qualitative in nature. Continuing survey of both these elites, and an understanding of the relationship between public and elite opinion, will be necessary as Canadians continue to work through these important issues.

Differences by age and region

Such differences between public and elite opinion are also echoed in differences among other subgroups in the population. In discussions, recipients of services were more likely to be protective in wanting to maintain government programs. As users, they relied on elements of the social safety net, felt they were already doing their utmost to get by, and worried about others who might fall through the cracks. Randomly recruited participants were more likely to take a "tough love" approach calling for steeper cuts and quicker action. In considering deeper consequences, these positions often modified in both directions. Recipients began to articulate ways in which the net could become a springboard and randomly recruited Canadians began to work through the assumption that cuts alone could solve problems and move to a position that approved more transitional forms of support.

Age appeared to be a potential factor in these differences, and 1994 polling data confirm this observation. Recipients of services are younger and more vulnerable for that reason alone, given the difficulties faced by the under 25 generation in entering today's labour force. Polling data suggest that younger Canadians on the whole tend to be somewhat more protective of the safety net and empathetic to the difficulties of those in needs, as are those with only some high school education. They also think we need to talk about providing more, not less generous benefits (Table 10).

Differences by region also exist in views of social programs, but with a significant sense of contradiction about what people really want. Based again on 1994 data, Albertans are less likely to see social programs as effective, and more likely to see them as making people dependent. They do not agree, however, that the quality and accessibility of programs should be reduced in order to reduce taxes. Quebecers like the security of social programs, worry less about the deficit, and tend to be concerned about hurting those who really need programs. Nevertheless, they also want people to take more responsibility for themselves. Residents of Atlantic Canada are the only Canadians who say we should be talking about providing more rather than less generous program benefits (Table 10).

Achieving national objectives

In considering governments' roles, Canadians attach importance to national consistency and equity. In July/August 1995, 60% of Canadians agreed that Canadians have a right to expect a minimum level of service wherever they live, including 66% of Albertans but only 48% of Quebecers. Only 36% felt that provinces are best able to decide what services are needed, with most residents in most provinces agreeing only about 32% of the time, and Quebecers agreeing 49% of the time (Table 20).

These views of national standards vary for different forms of social programs. In July/August 1995, 94% of Canadians saw standards as essential in health care (80% as very essential), 88% as essential in university/college education (56% as very essential), and 78% as essential in social assistance (but only 36% as very essential). Respectively, only 2, 4, and 6% said that standards were not at all essential (Table 21).

Canadians are uncertain, however, about how to resolve the jurisdictional issues surrounding the development of national standards: 54% agree that failing an agreement with the provinces, the federal government should establish the standards itself and withhold money from provinces that do not meet those standards. Strikingly, those in Atlantic Canada are most in agreement at 70% (Table 22).

Unfortunately, the division of responsibility is not an issue that has been widely covered in the polling data available for this report. Nevertheless, there is also some evidence to suggest that within the context of national standards, Canadians do not hold strong views of actual jurisdictional responsibility. For example, while 51% see job training and counselling as resting with the provinces, 26% see this as a federal responsibility, and 20% think it should be a shared responsibility. Similarly, 42% see social assistance and social services as provincial, but 35% see it as a federal responsibility, and 20% see it as a shared one (Table 23). In terms of health care, Canadians may be returning to a view of federal responsibility. In 1991, 51% saw it as a provincial responsibility, 35% as federal, and 8% as shared. In 1992, the support for provincial jurisdiction had dropped to 38%, while that for federal moved to 44% and for shared responsibility to 15% (Table 24).

These views on national standards suggest that Canadians are still working through many issues with regard to jurisdiction and responsibility. Findings from discussion groups concur. While participants addressing these issues voiced concerns about consistent levels of service and regional economic equity, they did not appear to have a clear picture of jurisdictional issues. Some suggested that the provinces should start working together on common interests, but many also seemed to think that the federal government had an important role to play. Most often, they focused on the substance of the debate on social programs, rather than on issues related to federalism and the division of powers. Like respondents in polls then, participants seemed to want national consistency, but were less certain how to achieve it in the face of provincial disagreement. Sometimes they focused in on the need for community decision making as a way of guaranteeing consistency of services, but usually came back to the need for some more cohesive exercise that could set common objectives for all to aim for. These issues are clearly ones that Canadians will need to address more deeply in an ongoing public dialogue.

Dealing with waste and inefficiency

While Canadians want government to assist those in need, they are uncertain and ambivalent about new directions, priorities and principles for policy in social programs. In polls, Canadians are particularly sceptical of government for not managing better; based on 1994 data, trust in the federal government's ability to reform social programs runs extremely low (Table 25). Many Canadians are angry about the abuses and failures of current systems. They are deeply concerned about current levels of government expenditure and want programs to be more effective and efficient. Discouraged by inertia, Canadians are voting for governments that offer the image of change. This explains some of the differences between recent election results and the overall findings of this study. In their last votes, Albertans and Ontarians have embraced parties offering guarantees focused on efficiency and effectiveness, seeing these as essential and realizable goals in the context of deficit reduction. In polls and public judgment exercises, Canadians stress the need for greater accountability and efficiency in government, but they also do not want to lose essential social programs.

While Canadians are concerned about waste and inefficiency, and committed to restructuring their social programs to support individual self-reliance, they do not want to base these decisions solely on the fiscal bottom line. They hold firm to the notion of government expenditure reductions, but are looking for alternatives to simple slash-and-burn responses. This is reflected in scepticism in the public's view of the motivations of the federal government behind social program reform. In 1994, only 27% of Canadians felt that they genuinely wanted to improve program efficiency and effectiveness, compared to 61% who saw it as a cost-cutting exercise, and 9% who saw both as motivations. Strikingly, young Canadians are more likely to see cost reduction as the motive (Table 26).

Difficult economic times appear to catalyze a stronger concern and interest in collective responses through government. At the same time, Canadians do not approve of how government currently carries out its responsibilities. Where they are frustrated with government, it is not in the range of programs to assist those in need, but in the ways those programs are delivered and organized. Canadians do not necessarily want less government, but better government.

In discussion groups, participants worked through options that called for a systemic consideration of new directions and a strategic reorientation of systems and structures. In education, for instance, a basic belief in accessibility remains strong, but more than ever Canadians want the system to deliver on its promises of quality and relevance. For health care, Canadians' commitment to universality is often qualified by concerns about the system's cost, the abuse and overuse of services, and debates about user fees. When the discussion turns to concerns about income security, most Canadians call for more stringent criteria and the creation of incentives, but they want assurances that government responses will be compassionate.

Changing Family Realities

Canadians are ambivalent about changing family and work values. They want to ensure that all able-bodied residents join the workforce, but they also want children to enjoy the benefits of good parenting.

"I believe so strongly in prevention and I think if you don't support young children to a level above the poverty line, then they will in turn grow up to be the young adults who need help as well because they won't have gotten through school."

In 1993, only 16% of Canadians said they had no sense of personal responsibility to be involved in the lives of children who are not their own (Table 27) and saw parenting as one of our biggest challenges. At the same time, children were seen primarily as the responsibility of parents, with older Canadians taking a more detached stance (Table 27). Feelings about whether parents receive enough help or support are mixed; one third say they do not, but one quarter think they do (Table 28). Similarly, while 30% would be willing to pay more for programs and services to help parents raise their children, 38% disagree (Table 29). Many Canadians also seem to expect sole support parents, even those with very young children, to combine work and family responsibilities rather than stay on social assistance. At the same time, almost 60% would welcome a proposal to support one parent in two-income families to stay at home with his or her children (Table 30).

"Most governments are only in power for four years so they don't care about long-term things. They just care about four years. And they can't look at putting money into this two-year old and thinking, if I take good care of this two-year old then they won't end up on assistance or in jail when they get to be eighteen because that's too long an age for most governments to think."

Discussion group participants gave little recognition to the double bind these conflicting imperatives put on individuals and families, or to the individual and collective financial ramifications. Few initially acknowledged the gap between what they thought should happen and what families can afford. For example, some participants championed a movement to pressure families to work at minimum wage employment to be self-reliant. They did not take into account that at minimum wage it would be impossible for one parent to remain at home: two salaries would be needed to survive.

Family reliance

To assign responsibility and, particularly, to cut costs, discussion group participants espoused the value of family reliance as a first resort. Some looked to a past where people could turn to their family rather than the government for assistance. In resolving their conflicts over these values, participants struggled to define reasonable expectations in new circumstances. Participants held on to an ideal of self-sufficient families, but acknowledged as discussion evolved that changing times have diminished the number of broader family, inter-generational, and community supports for families.

Despite the emphasis participants placed on self-sufficiency, they also advocated moving away from family supports to find employment; they did so without weighing the risk of increased isolation or increased dependency on government if a move does not result in a job. Indeed, participants often lamented the loss of family supports. They tended to see families unlike their own as failing to live up to

"You're absolutely responsible for the choices you make. It's just that some people have less choices and they don't have this much opportunity. If you're one of the fortunate, that have more choices to choose from, you can make good ones or bad ones. But it's harder for the people that have a very small opportunity to choose from. But they're still responsible for the choices that they make."

traditional family values. Only after reflecting together on the changing workplace and new demands on families, were participants prepared to take a less punitive stance. In groups of social assistance recipients, participants noted that some individuals without family supports need to rely on something or someone else.

At-home care of children and elderly parents was considered by some as the ideal. Concern was high that "children of today" are not growing up with the same values as did participants. Family values often seemed to refer directly to traditional values such as "children obeying their elders." One common reason given for the absence of these values was that a parent (most often the mother) was not at home caring for the children.

With widely different meanings, the phrase "back to the basics" was used in a nostalgic refrain. It could mean appreciating the value of child-rearing when undertaken by a mother. It could also mean reductions so that only essential services are provided. Just as often, it evoked the ways in which participants felt that individuals, extended families, communities, and social programs should respond to the needs of families. These conflicting views suggest that a deeper debate about the relationship between the family and the state lay beneath the surface. Working through issues surrounding the value of families, without blaming particular families or individuals, took considerable time in many groups.

"Focus on children before everybody because they're our future. Think of the effect it will have in two generations from now."

"Not everybody has a family, not everybody has that support. So what happens to that woman if she does not have a supportive family?"

Coming to the recognition that family failures are societal deficits – rather than individual ones – defused a great deal of anger and uncertainty in discussion groups. When this happened, stereotypes faded, the myth of traditional, self-sufficient families broke down, and the discussion changed focus. Both the limitations of some traditional families, including instances of authoritarianism and abuse, and the successes of some non-traditional families, were recognized.

In working through these issues, it appears that Canadians will continue to value families, but also examine the strengths and weaknesses of a whole range of family types. In that context, participants were also much more prepared to struggle with solutions that are compassionate and effective. Participants began to acknowledge that families have always relied on extended family help, community ties, and, to a lesser degree, state supports through the tax system, education, recreation, health, housing and other areas. Most still wanted to achieve a form of

"It doesn't have to be a mother/father household, but a stable household will help to bring the family values on line."

"The family structure in the past – a couple of generations ago – was built strong because not only did we have mom or dad home, but we had aunts, we had uncles, we had grandparents. And where mom or dad was weak, we had that resource there to keep it strong. Our families are not like that. It's very unfortunate when we have single-parent families, but the stress put on us as parents because of that breakdown of family structure reflects into our society a great deal."

family reliance as a first resort, but they were more prepared to acknowledge that an overly idealized notion of family self-sufficiency is not a useful basis for social policy development.

This project has only taken a first step in developing a constructive dialogue to resolve the conflicts and contradictions that Canadians experience in the relationship between families and the state. This dialogue must be fostered in the context of how Canadians wish to engage in cooperation and social cohesion. As the discussions on governance and partnerships in later chapters of this report suggest, the groundwork is now being laid for a more sustained dialogue on families, interdependence, and our broader social institutions.

Responsibility for children

Based on 1993 data, Canadians value children "in their own right, not just because they will grow up to become productive adults" (Table 28). Often this commitment stays at an abstract level, however. Given the lack of resolution about family complexity, Canadians remain uncertain about how to realize this priority.

Discussion group participants expressed a broad sense of collective responsibility for children. Many saw children as the future of the country and, therefore, the most important investment, which led them to propose options that they saw as forward-looking and preventive. Child development initiatives to ensure that every child realizes his or her full potential were said to be high priorities.

"It's better to have someone at home with the children – mother or father, uncle or aunt, grandparents – because they share values, so you are constantly putting to the young person."

"I think that if you decide to have children, somebody should be at home all the time."

"They should go to work like everyone else."

Participants were, however, hesitant to provide state support that might in any way interfere with parental authority. Beyond basic health care and education for all children, only in exceptional circumstances, such as child abuse or neglect, did most wish to intervene directly in children's lives.

With a strong value that children should remain primarily the responsibility of families, discussion group participants wanted to exercise the collective will by supporting parents. For example, in examining a proposed tradeoff on the more appropriate way to provide school lunches to needy children, participants rejected both options – direct funding or part-

"A lot of them will have a few more kids because their welfare cheque will get bigger."

"A young girl says, 'I want to get away from my mother and father, I want to get out of here, so I'll get pregnant, get my own apartment and go on welfare'."

nerships to foster indirect funding – presented to them. They tended to blame parents for their inadequacies and failures to provide for their children. However, because they didn't want to see children suffer, they were willing to construct a third option that would provide parents with better parenting and budgeting skills.

As much as these Canadians wanted to address the needs of children, unresolved images of families as isolated and self-sufficient left discussion group participants feeling helpless. Only a few participants, out of personal experience, said that they believe the state should take a larger role for children of all ages. They felt that children should be considered individuals and not their parents' property.

These conflicting viewpoints on children demonstrate the fundamental dilemmas Canadians face in valuing collective investment in children. Caught between values that stress an almost mythical ideal of the family as a private, self-sufficient, and autonomous entity, and a dawning recognition of the complexities and interdependencies of families and the state, participants seemed to be stymied on how best to foster child development and youth independence. While they felt sure about intervening to protect children when a family fails, they had difficulty defining a more preventive and future-oriented role that could build on the value of collective responsibility without infringing on parental rights. More discussion is needed to reconcile the view of the autonomous family with that of society's collective responsibility to promote the well-being of all children.

Working Through Conflicts and Trade-Offs

As a result of the conflicts and contradictions in their desires to retain social programs and achieve fiscal responsibility, most Canadians were eager to work through necessary trade-offs to realize an optimal level of well-being. Recognizing that the country is going to change and that cuts are inevitable, Canadians are rethinking or working their way through conflicts in priorities. They are cautious in making cuts, assertive in demanding proof that programs are well conceived and efficiently managed, and willing to debate carefully the values and principles that will guide decisions about cuts.

Canadians are angry; each end of the income ladder blames the other for the problems confronting society. Those at the top feel they are paying more than their fair share, while those at the bottom feel increasingly trapped and helpless in the face of forces outside their control. The "haves" tend to blame the "have-nots" for welfare fraud, unnecessary uses of services, and general laziness and lack of motivation. Those among "have-nots" tend to blame the wealthy and powerful for selfishness, and blame whoever is further down the scale, including criminals and rip-off artists, for defrauding a system that they really need. Everyone attacks government for incompetence.

Going beyond simplistic solutions

Faced with difficult trade-offs and encouraged to listen thoughtfully and engage in a process of "second thoughts," discussion group participants struggled to clarify their core values, work through conflicts and contradictions, and resolve value dilemmas. Ambivalence surfaced over the course of discussions of key trade-

"Canadians are becoming more and more individualistic and concerned only for their own welfare and how much tax they pay. That's losing touch with the fact that my welfare and well-being depend on the well-being of other Canadians."

offs. Participants often softened harsh or punitive stances as they considered the impacts of their initial choices on fellow Canadians. For every call to "get back to the basics," an equal and more reflective debate ensued about the changing dynamics of families, the disappearance of old jobs without equivalent replacements, and the forces of globalization confronting Canada. Through the dialogue, Canadians affirmed or strengthened some long-standing principles, explored and sometimes rejected others, and refined those that required renewal.

Canadians are often unwilling to choose between tough alternatives, sometimes because they do not want to relinquish cherished programs, but also because they do not feel available alternatives achieve desired objectives. Faced with what they saw as unsatisfactory options, discussion group participants exhibited a fierce drive to articulate alternatives or third options that more closely reflect the nuances of complex value dilemmas. Their ambivalence and frustration with simple solutions was reflected in the sophistication they brought to the analysis of problems and solutions. They were not willing to simplify the discussion and instead worked through complex issues by identifying connections and underlying causes, and especially by linking economic and social objectives. Most often, they developed multifaceted solutions focused on underlying causes and looked for comprehensive strategies to prevent future problems rather than just solve existing problems.

"People are feeling unheard, they feel like they don't know what is going on and they don't have any say. We should know where our money is being spent. I would like to see the budget."

Canadians are demanding new forms of democratic engagement

As discussions unfold, it becomes clear that Canadians do not feel that they have been adequately consulted in the process of defining the changes that are about to take place. Despite disillusionment with current forms of consultation, they have begun to demand new forms of democratic engagement. The Canadians consulted for this report wanted to find new ways to influence the decision-making process with regard to social policy. As a reflection of their frustration with the limited vision and effectiveness of government, they want new ways to participate and engage in the political process, more information, and a clearer sense that government will report back to them. These demands are new.

On almost every issue, Canadians demand greater accountability and transparency from politicians, public servants, and citizens. They call for more partnerships and greater involvement across all sectors. In the last federal

"Governments have got to be honest and moral in their decisions. To change a law or not change a law just because of money is ridiculous."

"I don't think that our provincial government has their finger on the pulse of the people. I don't think they understand how people feel. Ultimately, it's the dollars. I think there should be a lot of concern there. When they're finished, we're going to have a lot more expenditures trying to clean the mess they are creating."

"I think they're cutting in the wrong areas. They're cutting education, which affects the young, and health services, which affects older people. They should be influenced by the overall good of the people. They have a moral responsibility to observe the good of all people, not just financially but healthwise and every way."

election, Canadians also sought to achieve accountability by voting in the party that promised change.

Social policy reform requires a new process of democratization and development at both the personal and societal level, as the reform process leads Canadians to redefine themselves and their national identity. While they agree that they may no longer be able to hold on to any "sacred cows" in social policy, they also demand the information and engagement necessary to ensure that the process of change remains theirs, not just a product of fiscal agendas. They want new language, new tools, and new partnerships to help chart the territory of social policy reform.

For this project, social assistance recipients and Canadians selected randomly worked through these issues separately. Social assistance recipients preferred to voice their concerns in a "safe" environment, which was provided by social agencies cooperating with this study. In future discussions, it will be important to consider opportunities to bring these two groups together to work through the issues and benefit from mutual exposure. Understanding the values and empathizing with the experiences of others were important factors in reaching resolution on some of the key issues of this study. The process needs to be fostered to encourage better public information and discussion on public policy priorities and trade-offs.

2. Canadians' Value Statements: Social Assistance Programs

Polling data suggests that Canadians see government social programs as last resorts. While they support a broad range of other roles for government, 7 in 10 also see a role in providing "the base minimal presence in order to allow people to get on with their own affairs." This view of government as promoter and protector does not, however, diminish Canadians' sense of personal autonomy. Most agree that "people are responsible for their own lives" and must save for their own retirement (Table 16).

"I'm not saying there is a lot of work, but you should take whatever there is to take."

"I know a man who has cerebral palsy. I can't imagine him doing anything. So do we say, 'Because you can't do a thing, you don't deserve a minimum standard of living'?"

In addition, a majority of Canadians agree that "if people just took more responsibility for themselves and their families we wouldn't need all of these social programs" (Table 31). In 1994, three in four Canadians agreed that "more and more people are going to have to stop depending on our federal government and learn to fend for themselves" (Table 32).

Self-Reliance

Canadians differ in the degree to which they recognize systemic factors that limit an individual's choices and accomplishments. For most, collective responsibility enters in only when personal effort fails. For a few, the limits are restricted to actual disability or impairment.

Participants' differences in the emphasis they placed on collective and individual responsibility reflected their own experiences. Agency-recruited groups, whose participants had lower incomes and fewer jobs, were more likely to embrace a stronger direct role for government. Randomly recruited groups, whose members were more likely to be employed and who had higher incomes, thought government

"She needs to be taught, 'Hey, you can't spend your $30 a month on tobacco, and you can't drink. You need to change your lifestyle'."

"There should only be a small number of kids that need food. The money that they give: GST and the child tax credit and all the stuff I would get, it's ridiculous. I mean, the things you read in the paper, what they spend on luxuries, I could feed twelve people for what they spend on three people. It's ridiculous. We shouldn't see that many kids go to school hungry."

"The responsibility is for each individual to be aware of where we are going with our lives

should play a strong role but put more onus on individual responsibility.

Participants who had never used the system were more likely to believe that people on social assistance lacked motivation or were "lazy." They also worried that even minimum levels of income have allowed some recipients to afford luxuries, including cigarettes, liquor, and bingo. Some felt this means that welfare levels are too high, particularly if they appear to enable recipients to afford items not accessible to the working poor. At other times, they worry that income is misspent as recipients indulge habits rather than provide nourishing meals for their children.

and also to increase awareness for everybody else – through education – not to always look for the government to be the answer, because that's why we are in such a deficit."

While some participants held on to these angry judgments even after lengthy discussion, most moved to more empathetic positions. They began to explore the reasons that able-bodied adults might not be able to find work, including the lack of available jobs, low self-confidence, lack of skills for jobs that cover their bills, wishes to parent children full-time, and other reasons. Even within these limits, some felt that they only had a responsibility to take care of themselves, their families, their close friends, and perhaps their neighbours.

Those who used the social assistance system were less likely to blame the individual for failure and more likely to identify a range of external factors that limit choices and therefore self-reliance. These included age, social and personal background, income level, race, and caring for young children at home.

What Are the State's Responsibilities?

One core value expressed by all participants is to ensure that the "deserving" are not negatively affected by the country's need to get its fiscal house in order. Within this responsibility, however, participants were uncertain about how to judge others as worthy or unworthy of support. Strikingly, individuals often seemed to draw the line at their own situations: anyone making as much effort as I is deserving, anyone making less effort is undeserving.

"A lot of people were brought up in abusive homes. Beaten up. Alcoholism. And they are sitting there drinking alcohol because their parents did. They're beating up people because their parents did. They have to get some help along the way to get on the right track."

"I don't have a problem with someone receiving social assistance, but if they are capable of working, then I say that they should be working."

Social assistance recipients and employed Canadians differed on whether the state had a responsibility for helping "the working poor." The first group saw transitional supports

"I think I am being responsible; I am doing my part. Why is this person just allowed to get away with this at my expense?"

for people earning minimum wages as legitimate. People working at that wage seemed to feel that assisting them would *not* be legitimate. They were much more likely to target any form of social assistance as problematic. Both groups were struggling, but had different views of what might offer a reasonable platform to reduce that struggle. Both groups, however, resented those who were better off and did not "really have to work" or those who did not understand the struggles they faced.

In working through these issues, many participants were uncertain about how to resolve conflicting beliefs. The problem surfaced not only between population subgroups, but also between individuals at all income levels. By the end of every discussion on income security, almost all participants had refined their original positions and had personally categorized those who "deserved" assistance and those who did not. Most participants were willing to broaden their original definitions of "deserving" to include people who had made an honest attempt at becoming financially self-reliant but who were failing. For example, one participant who had started with vehement comments about welfare recipients altered her perspective considerably after discussion.

Abuse of the Social Security System

While Canadians hold differing views on the intended beneficiaries of social assistance, most agree that society must place a priority on dealing with abuse in the social assistance system. In 1994, the vast majority believed that social programs create dependency and complacency on the part of beneficiaries (Table 33). And only one in three agreed that stories about cheating in the welfare system are exaggerated.

Many discussion group participants believed that the government should put a high priority on ridding the system of abuse, which all saw as extremely widespread. This was a topic where people were not willing to listen to other points of view. Even when a fellow participant would attempt to put forward figures of much reduced rates of welfare fraud, most group members would not consider them seriously.

Fairness was central to the values of participants. Members of every group expressed anger towards individuals who were cheating the system. Also, in their minds, preventing abuse would free up funds for other activities.

Only a couple of participants felt that the focus should be different, for example, moving from concentrating on welfare fraud by the poor to concentrating on tax or corporate fraud by the rich.

Encouraging Personal Autonomy

For Canadians, the crux of balancing individual and state responsibility, and of avoiding abuse and cutting costs, lies in reshaping income security systems to offer incentives and encourage personal autonomy. Canadians become hostile toward individuals they perceive as dependent because of a lack of motivation,

"I've had it! I've worked darn hard, maybe things haven't always gone my way, maybe I haven't gotten everything I want, I'm pretty happy, I have some bad days, but most of my days are good. But by God! It really makes me mad when I see people saying, 'You owe me. I do nothing, but you owe me'."

but most also recognize that this situation is engendered by flaws in the system. Participants in both kinds of groups frequently quoted the homily, "*Give a man a fish and you feed him for a day. Teach a man to fish and you feed him for the rest of his life.*"

Many Canadians believe that the programs themselves, as currently structured, can exacerbate problems (Tables 34 and 35). For example, a majority believe that welfare can be a disincentive by "killing" initiative. This belief is also found, though to a lesser extent, in the area of Unemployment Insurance. In a 1989 survey, more than half of the population agreed that "the present system of unemployment insurance encourages people not to work" (data not shown). Canadians believe that programs are open to abuse and can often undermine the goal they are designed to achieve. As will be seen in Chapter 3, "Canadians' Value Statements: Social Programs," discussion group members feel even more vehemently about this issue today.

One popular proposal to deal with abuse and wastage is to focus social assistance on program supports, rather than income provision. For example, fully 9 in 10 Canadians believed in 1992 that "money by itself will not solve the problems of poverty and social inequality and governments would be far better off to give the poor access to education, day care and the opportunities that would allow them to stand on their own two feet" (Table 36). However, Quebecers, those with less education, and those in the lowest income quintile are somewhat more likely to want to "provide more income" (Table 37). Close to half of Canadians, told in a 1992 survey question that most people do not see money itself as the solution, agreed that emphasizing programs will decrease the number of people receiving social assistance for long periods of time; 2 in 10 thought that a shift to programs would create little change and 3 in 10 said it would lead to increases in use of social assistance over the long haul (Table 36).

"It seems there is so much abuse from people just sitting back and taking handouts rather than doing something about it or taking an opportunity to change their life, like getting into one of those retraining programs, rather than saying 'Oh! no, I can't do that,' and making excuses as to why."

"A lot of energy is wasted arguing about the supposed abuse of social assistance. I don't think that anybody wants to live on social assistance. You try living on the amount you get on social assistance; it is no kind of a life. Some people are trapped in this downward spiral, are just gasping for breath and can't get out of it, but way more money is wasted in our national expenditure than is consumed by the abuse of social assistance."

"I know people that sit on welfare and sell drugs on the side – but still collect welfare cheques. No, I don't agree that we should serve these people. But that's why the system is failing. There are too many people taking advantage of it."

"How do you define minimum? Does that mean that you have inadequate housing, poor access to social services and to health care, because that's what seems to be happening here, especially in the province of New Brunswick. You'd be shocked to see the conditions that people live in, in this city. We have the lowest rates for welfare."

"Every Canadian should have the right to <u>earn</u> a minimum standard of living."

All Canadians place a high priority on developing a system of income supports that is realistic. Integration and incentives are crucial to everyone. Canadians who have not used income supports tend to take relatively harsher stances. They appear to be just beginning to separate their anger towards those they see as misusing or abusing that system from their frustration at the flaws in the income support system itself. They are just beginning to come to terms with the fact that a system set up as a stopgap measure for an unfortunate few has become, in a troubled economic climate, the only recourse for a much larger population, including growing numbers of women and children after divorce, a large cohort of younger Canadians trying to enter the labour market in the midst of recession, and many recently discouraged and dispossessed workers whose unemployment benefits have expired without new jobs appearing on the scene.

Guaranteed annual income

This is also consistent with surveys over recent years that report a drop in support for proposals for a guaranteed annual income. In polls in the early 1980s, most Canadians favoured a guaranteed annual income (Table 38). While the proportion in favour peaked in the mid-1980s, by 1991 close to 7 in 10 expressed support. In a 1994 survey, in which the context for the guaranteed annual income was very different, only 1 in 3 Canadians accepted the concept (Table 39). The tough times of the 1990s may have made Canadians more resistant to certain forms of entitlement.

In discussions, the question of a guaranteed annual income received strong support from a segment of group participants who believed that it should be a compassionate right of all Canadians. They also believed it would raise dignity and prevent the negative stigma attached to social assistance.

However, whether all Canadians, "deserving" or not, should have a minimum standard of living was a question hotly debated in the discussions groups. Those hesitant to provide a guaranteed standard of living feared that it would be too expensive for taxpayers, that it would take away motivation to work, and that the "undeserving" would receive the benefit regardless of their actions. The perceived lack of effort and dependency of recipients of income support triggered negativity and hostility in

"If my 16-year-old daughter came home pregnant, she should not have the right to get an apartment and go [...] I should have some responsibility of taking care of her and her child, make sure her education is continued so she can be a single mom growing up. Our family values then are still embedded into not only our 16 year old child but also in our grandchild."

"I would like to see something in the Constitution specifically for children – anyone under the age of 18 – that they have their bill of rights, they have the right to housing, to not be beaten, to not be sexually or mentally abused, and if that is the case, then they can go and get a lawyer and divorce their parents and choose their own foster parents."

"When they're 14 or 15, they don't have the maturity and the background to make their own decisions."

"If you're pulling somebody out of an abusive situation, where their life is in jeopardy, and their basic needs are not being met, this is a whole lot better than not knowing whether you're going to walk out of your house alive the next day. Because that does happen, that's a fact."

"Not every 14-year-old person wants to go into a foster home or a group home. You have to look at that individual, their maturity, their

group discussions, especially among members of randomly recruited groups. Among those in contact with social service agencies, the discussion more often focused on the context of labour market slowdowns and the barriers to labour market participation.

background, whether or not there are family supports, because there are kids that come from homes that are totally dysfunctional. In one case a young person might be able to go live with an aunt or an uncle or a relative, but maybe that's just not possible here."

Should teenagers be eligible for social assistance?

When discussing whether teenagers should be eligible to receive social assistance directly at the age of 14 or 18, most participants felt it was important for families to take responsibility for their children until the age of 18. Only in extraordinary circumstances should the state step in. Participants agreed that allowing youth to receive social assistance directly would encourage some to leave home, whereas the best solution might be to try to work out problems with their parents. They also objected to the state providing cash payments to minors on the grounds that it was contrary to the values of work, self-discipline and self-reliance. In cases where a young person could not remain with his or her parents (for example, because of abuse) they recommended that the state take a more active role by placing the individual with foster parents or in a group home.

Participants who felt that 14-year-olds should be able to receive social assistance directly, with eligibility determined on a case-by-case basis, were most often in the agency-recruited groups. They drew on personal experiences either as teenagers who did not remain with their parents, and who suffered from being moved from foster home to foster home, or as parents who had taken in runaway teens. They believed that some teenagers would benefit from the stable independence that social assistance would provide.

Workfare

Frustrations about welfare go back many years in public opinion polls. Even in 1962, a Gallup survey found that nearly 8 in 10 Canadians believed that "employable men" should be required to take any available work to receive relief assistance – our modern notion of "workfare" (Table 40). By the mid-1970s, the proportion supporting workfare had increased to close to 9 in 10. In 1993, this view held steady (Table 41).

"I'd like to see more emphasis on the positive aspects to eliminate that welfare spiral [...] and to find different ways to get people back on stream so they are in the flow of life and not off to the side."

"Taking more of an individual look. I mean I know you can't look at a hundred million Canadians individually but comparing a single mom to somebody who's 20 years old and capable of working and is just sitting there collecting."

Participants realized that implementing workfare in itself will not achieve fundamental reforms. The more fundamental challenge for government is to restore incentives to the system. Many Canadians feel it is unreasonable to expect someone who barely survives on social assistance to manage a family with a minimum-wage job that offers no benefits or security. Without incentives to work, support in the transition to the labour force, and solutions regarding child care, many see it as unlikely that the situation of social assistance recipients will be changed solely by making people work for welfare. Instead, the cycle of dependency will be increased.

"I don't really think they should just give out welfare. I think people should work for it. Stop teaching these people that it's okay to received money for free. No. Show them that they have to work for it. It will give them some pride in themselves to work for this money. I don't care if it's sweeping the street. I don't care what it is. But give them some pride."

Requiring people to work in exchange for social assistance benefits was popular with participants of randomly recruited groups. This idea received support not because participants thought it could reduce the overall cost of social assistance to the state, but rather because it was consistent with the value of self-reliance and fairness. The underlying value appeared to be that people should never "receive something for nothing" because it would breed dependency and destroy one's work ethic and pride. Participants also agreed that the experience gained by recipients could help to prepare them for jobs.

At the same time, some participants indicated that workfare is only a partial answer to the problem. This closely parallelled the views of participants in agency-recruited groups who want employment that pays a living wage – or at least that does not fall below social assistance standards. Otherwise, they could be taking low-wage, low-security jobs and losing the ability to cover rents, food, and medical costs for their children.

Single Mothers Receiving Social Assistance

Many participants were concerned not only about direct welfare fraud, but also about what they considered misuses of the system by those who could work. For instance, a married couple, holding down two low-wage jobs while juggling family responsibilities, might level charges of abuse at single mothers who accepted social assistance. These cases were labelled unfair use of the system. Protests by other group members who had used social assistance at one time or another, or personal stories of being on welfare for a short period and then finding work, were dismissed as the exception, not the rule. People targeted those whom they considered "deserved" and "did not deserve" assistance.

In contrast, single mothers on welfare saw themselves as legitimate recipients of social assistance. If they charged anyone for abuse of the system, it was "drug dealers" and others earning unreported income who might be able to work. They saw these individuals as taking resources that were supposed to be available to help them and their children. Sole

"Walk a mile in my shoes and see how you feel about it."

"Maybe it's not so easy to say, or to decide, after all. Unless you walk a mile in their shoes, how do you know?"

support mothers also felt these cases gave others a sense that all welfare recipients were corrupt.

"I'm on income assistance. Society is taking care of me. But eventually, I plan to go back to work, after I parent my child a bit more. But it takes a while to gain confidence again. So, I'm trying to go a step at a time."

Most sole support mothers were shocked and disturbed by the notion that they were abusing the system. They felt the stigma of being on welfare, but they saw themselves as in crisis, and fully expected to join the labour market when their children reached school age. They too often saw themselves as making maximum effort to raise children and make ends meet on what they described as next to nothing. They talked about the difficulties of watching every penny and the guilt of not being able to feed and provide for their children.

Single mothers unable to find work felt stymied by the view that they could do more or that they might be abusing the system. Many single mothers on social assistance also expressed the belief that it was important for them to be at home with their young children. They wanted people to be more sensitive to their situations as divorced women in their twenties trying to get back on their feet, rather than stereotyping them as unmarried teenage mothers. Some of them pointed out that the social assistance system had been set up precisely to help people like them. They couldn't see how they could possibly cope with jobs and young children in the current labour market.

"How can you motivate people on welfare to work when they know that they can make more on welfare than they can at Wal-Mart. It doesn't make sense. A lot of them aren't going to work. The people that are having the hardest problems today are the working poor. The people who are standing behind the cash register at Wal-Mart and K-mart."

"[Social assistance] is a program to be used to get you through a situation, but then you get off, you get on with your life and you get moving. You don't stay on it. That is not the purpose, that is the abuse."

"Many people just take advantage of it, and the ones who desperately need it don't get enough."

One or two women, however, confessed to their own abuse of the system. Unable to cope on the amount received on welfare, they told of earning small amounts of unreported income to bridge expenses.

For a few participants, expressions of frustration and anger at abusers of income security systems stopped at punishing the guilty. For the vast majority of participants, however, these concerns fuelled discussions about problems with the system itself and ideas for reform.

Single motherhood is the most contentious situation raised in discussions of people who "deserve" support. Many participants were intolerant of single parents on social assistance, and especially vehement about mothers who have more children while receiving social assistance. Some participants initially suggested that, to prevent this from occurring again, various individual freedoms should be suspended when individuals failed to take responsibility for themselves.

With deeper discussion, participants often softened these harsh solutions by considering the complexity of the situation of single mothers. They explored more systemic solutions, including finding ways to enforce child support payments and ensure child care supports.

As they explored these issues more deeply, participants began to realize that people on social assistance may already in fact be doing their best. They still focused on fairness, insisting that everyone able to work should work, but they were more willing to take into account the complex circumstances faced by parents raising children on their own. This suggests that definitions and standards of personal responsibility can change in discussion, and that resolution on the situation of "welfare mothers" may be possible as Canadians consider whether it is reasonable and fair to expect single parents with young children to join the labour market, or if we need to consider other options for assisting individuals in this situation.

A compelling insight on this issue came after a discussion leader was asked by participants in a randomly recruited group where she was going next. Instead of saying the next city, she strayed from her role as a facilitator to reply that her group that evening would consist of social assistance recipients, many of them single mothers on social assistance, who would be very disturbed by some of the labels attached to them that afternoon, including descriptions of them as "lazy" and "leeches." The facilitator said that these women saw themselves as struggling against difficult odds to find work and manage young children. The group's reaction, after the harsh judgments of the earlier discussion, was newly compassionate: *"But that's all we want for them too – a chance to do their best."*

Canadians want to be fair to those who are in need of income supports. 1994 polling data shows that 7 in 10 see a role for government in the redistribution of wealth (Table 19). They also clearly resist the notion that reform of the safety net should be made at unfair costs to individuals. As noted earlier, 71% are worried about those who will be harmed as changes are put into effect. (Table 10).

When our social assistance system was constructed, sole support parents were seen to fall squarely in the category of those who deserve support. Early motherhood was deemed a period when women would legitimately take a hiatus from the labour force in order to raise children. Divorce did not change that expectation. Today, although many of them work only part-time, women with very young children are more likely to work than not. The stay-at-home mother has become the exception rather than the rule.

"Aren't we the reason the system was set up? Isn't it supposed to help us and our children?"

"I don't know how anybody could live solely on welfare. I am having a really hard time with that. I have had to start doing something that is not legal and I don't like doing it because I want to set a good example for my daughter. I have no other way."

"If that person down the road decides to have three children and two of them are taken into care, and she decides to have another one and goes and has another one, I don't think it is my responsibility to take care of her children because she is not responsible for herself. I think there is a limit."

"If women are left on their own with a couple of children to be supported, then the government has to look after them, but go after the other [parent] to help support them. I think they should be encouraged not to have any more children while they are on the system."

"Social services as opposed to dad paying support for his children. Why should I pay it when he's working and he can pay it?"

"I feel that I need to be home with my baby. And yet it's the taxpayers that are allowing me to be at home with my daughter."

This changing pattern of female labour force participation generates new expectations for women with children after divorce. Rather than relying on state assistance, most Canadians seem to want them to join the labour force and become self-supporting. The paradox resides in the fact that some women's work skills, the precarious state of the current labour market, and the nature of most women's jobs, do not permit them to earn a family wage, afford child care, and also fulfil their child-rearing responsibilities.

What is fair and unfair in these circumstances, and how Canadians want to define "a chance to do their best" remains open to question, and all of the alternatives have costs. If Canadians want sole support mothers to work, they must either provide more integrated transitional supports or run the risk that most of these women and their children will live even further below the poverty line than they do now. If they want to assist these women during a difficult period, Canadians must face the fact that the income security system will continue to have single parents and their children as its largest recipient group.

Alternatively, Canadians using income supports, especially mothers with young children, placed the emphasis for social assistance on ensuring dignity and compassion and on providing supportive transitions. They find themselves caught between two conflicting sets of demands. They are expected to achieve self-sufficiency through employment and to nurture their children, all with diminishing family and community supports. They are just beginning to articulate their own confusion at being blamed for making use of a system that they understood as the appropriate last resort in the circumstances in which they find themselves.

Getting Out of the System

No clear resolution emerged on a number of issues. Canadians are reluctant to deny benefits to the "truly needy," including individuals with a disability and those making an effort to become employed. Suggestions varied for how to create a more integrated system of program supports linked to incentives. In discussions, many participants initially leant towards punitive measures, but others wanted to consider positive ways of helping people leave social assistance. As third options were considered, participants moved to clarify their view of how a more comprehensive and staged system could foster autonomy.

Agency-recruited participants, especially single mothers, also wanted avenues to get off the system. Many felt that coping with the social assistance system itself was a burden and a

"If there were more courses in trades, or in school where they give something free to you; a year of course free instead of having to pay back. Because sometimes it's really hard to get a job' [...]"

"It's just going to end up with more and more people on assistance if you don't train them."

"I am glad that they are implementing an education program for people who need to upgrade their skills, but there should be a follow-up after that. There should be somebody there to guide, not just say, 'Your graduation is on that day, sayonara'."

"Of course I would work if I could find it [...] but who will take care of my children, and how do I feed them on a minimum wage job?

barrier to autonomy, since they were seldom given the information, advice, or encouragement they needed to find jobs. Instead, they

I can't come home at the end of the week with $200 and support us."

felt doubly jeopardized by a system that labelled them as lazy, yet left them feeling powerless. Many talked about the stigmas attached to being on social assistance and the resulting low self-esteem. They wanted help to be provided compassionately, fairly, and with respect.

They also felt the hopelessness of making ends meet on social assistance when no jobs were available or when they saw no transition path to cope with a minimum wage job, child care costs, transportation, and all the other demands of trying to enter the labour market. With low assistance rates and low minimum wages, many of them felt trapped in the system and a few of them felt trapped into abusing it.

Training was seen by many as a step in the right direction, but many who had been through job training cycles complained that training seemed isolated from the world of work. Most importantly, links across social assistance, training, and employment were perceived as the keys to integration.

3. Canadians' Value Statements: Broad Social Programs

Through the 1980s, polls indicated that most Canadians supported a targeted rather than universal approach to government benefits in the abstract (Table 42). In 1993, half of those polled agreed that "government should not provide services to people who can pay for them out of their own pocket" (Table 43). A year later, Canadians appeared to be prepared, again in the abstract, to make trade-offs regarding quality and accessibility. This willingness to sacrifice programs breaks down, however, as polls probe specific kinds of cuts. And for each area of broad social policy, somewhat different implications must be drawn from polling as opposed to discussion group results.

As the program targets become more concrete, polls suggest that more people support universal accessibility. Canadians are open to cuts in the abstract, but resist specific cuts. Similarly, means testing is a reform that is likely to be resisted when it refers to specific, cherished programs. Perhaps for this reason, in discussion groups, the universality of health, education, and social programs was something many participants initially said they most valued about living in Canada. However, as discussions progressed, there was often consensus that the country could no longer afford universality in some areas. When facing tough choices about funding cuts, almost all participants advocated targeting public support in some way, usually by income. The traditional policy rationale for universality was not weighed by some participants, who considered it irrational to provide the same benefits and services to relatively well-off people and to those in need.

As participants came to resolution on appropriate targets, they placed greater emphasis on other principles that could guarantee accessibility. These included measures to ensure that programs would be accessible, fair, responsive, comprehensive, effective, and transparent.

"The ounce of prevention is worth a pound of cure. The dollar of prevention is worth ten dollars of the curing."

"Put [money] to something where it's going to be more productive for the whole, not just one little portion [...] where it benefits everyone."

"I travel throughout the States and other countries as well and I am very proud of the social system, the social safety net that we have here. I have met people in the States who will be in debt for the rest of their lives because a child happened to have had a sickness or injury or disease that required extensive hospital care. It was very sad to see these people in desperate situations that did not have the same resources that we have here."

"Whether you're the guy who is making that $5 or the guy that's making $100,000, people go to the hospital and receive the same care."

Health Care

Maintaining the accessibility of health care is a priority for Canadians. Many discussion group participants considered health care to be part of the foundation of Canadian identity.

Polls suggest that Canadians see health care as a "right" that all enjoy. In 1991, 3 in 4 Canadians said that free health care is a benefit that all Canadians *should* be eligible to receive (Table 44). In 1994, 6 in 10 Canadians believed that all people in Canada *have* equal access (Table 45).

"I know some people would have to cut down on the money they spend to allow for that, but the people that have babies that are handicapped – there is no way anybody that's on social assistance is going to be able to do it; they're going to be in debt their entire life just for a few years of the baby's life, and the baby could die. Who would want to be left with say $60,000 worth of doctor bills for a baby that may have died because of their illness, because they didn't get proper [treatment]?"

Canadians are likely to believe that access to health care could, in fact, be governed unfairly by inequities in income.

When asked to rate the importance of the five principles of the Canadian health care system, Canadians ranked "universality" first in 1991 and 1994 (Table 46). The importance attached to universality declined somewhat in that time, however, as did all of the other principles set out in the Canada Health Act: accessibility, portability, comprehensiveness, and public administration. In polls and discussions, the principle of accessibility – reasonable access without financial barriers – is often framed as a question of universality – eligibility for all residents in proportion to medical needs. In groups, while Canadians may often mistake the principle of universality for that of accessibility, their intent is nevertheless clear. They do not want to see a two-tier system that could disadvantage Canadians who cannot afford to pay or that would offer superior service to those at a financial advantage.

Within this basic value of health care as an entitlement of all, however, Canadians in discussions are willing to look for savings and priorities by identifying the most appropriate services to be funded. They accept that trade-offs will be necessary, but views on health care trade-offs are often polarized.

"Why would every child in the province need access to free resources, when [there are] lots of higher income or middle income parents that could afford it, and save the money for the people that couldn't?"

"What price do you put on a human life?"

User Fees

Along with the recent, slight weakening in support for accessibility in health care, polls also suggest that Canadians are increasingly prepared to support user fees as a way of providing additional funding for health care (Table 47). In 1992, a majority approved of the idea of user fees.

However, other research has indicated that support for user fees is directly linked to the amount of the fee: support is very high at nominal amounts and very low as the amount of the fee increases.

Some discussion group participants were willing to target health benefits by income, arguing that in the current environment, Canadians can no longer afford to hold on to "sacred cows." Targeting, however, goes hand in hand with the search for guarantees that it will not lead to any decline in basic service levels. In this sense, participants would compromise the accessibility of some services if they had guarantees of comparable benefits for all Canadians. For example, some participants chose to require parents who could afford it, to pay for immunizations for their children. They saw the middle class and wealthy as able to defray the cost of their medical treatment by paying user fees.

"At the end of the day, what will happen is that our health care is not effective, our children are not educated as well and they're not prepared as well as we need, and then there's a catch-up period. There's a cost then. What's motivating the country now is the cost and I think that cost is not going to be saved."

Canadians want user fees to deter abuses of the system due to inappropriate use, echoing their concerns about abuse and misuse of income security. They do not want fees to be a deterrent to those in genuine medical need, and still support free access to essential health care services regardless of income or other factors. In discussion groups, user fees also sometimes came up as a solution to an overburdened and expensive system, but participants did not specify the level of fee they would see as tolerable and made it clear that no one should be denied service. They wrestled with the burden of assessing need and administering a system based on means testing.

Even more fundamental debates emerged in discussions about other health issues, including trade-offs about:

- quality of life for the majority versus length of life for the terminally ill,
- centralized state-of-the-art services versus more regionalized basic services, and
- prevention versus remediation.

As in the polling data, participants were polarized.

"It is a really difficult choice. I am sure someone I know, some member of my family, is going to be in that cancer situation some day, but I still think the youth is just at that age that we have to help them [...]."

"I don't see the point in just surviving. Either there is a good life or there is no life. And that would be putting a higher strain on the health care which we are paying for people who are going to pass away regardless of what you do for them with the treatment."

Life prospects

Many discussion group participants considered it more important to achieve the greatest good for the greatest number rather than offering heroic services to a limited few. In some cases, this meant channelling education or preventive strategies to younger Canadians who will benefit over their lifetime, rather than attempting to prolong life in the case of terminal illness. However, this trade-off generated division, often leading participants to "agree to disagree." They seemed to realize that they would be unlikely to resolve these conflicts in a single discussion, or even in several discussions. In recognizing that others held conflicting but equally legitimate values, participants accepted that it may not always be possible to sway the deeply held values of others, and that at times resolving differences would require a vote and the denouement of the political process.

Regional versus central services

Similarly, views on decentralization of basic services versus highly centralized state-of-the-art services are highly polarized. Regionalized access to health services was most important to Canadians who had lived in smaller centres. When discussing a trade-off between funding one state-of-the-art cancer clinic in a major centre and six basic cancer clinics across the province, more chose to support the six clinics. They argued that:

- it would be difficult or impossible financially for some in need to travel to and stay in the major city;
- it was unfair for sick people to have to travel to obtain treatment; and
- it was more beneficial for people to stay near their families.

Participants who identified themselves as being from smaller centres were very conscious of barriers to accessibility because of distance. They considered it more important to maintain accessibility to an adequate, if not excellent, standard of care. However, about one half of participants were willing to trade off accessibility for the state-of-the-art cancer clinic. Maintaining the country's capacity to deliver world class treatment and conduct leading-edge research was considered to be more important than ensuring accessibility. In addition, these participants wished the best – not simply basic care – for loved ones. There was a firm belief that those needing treatment would be able to travel to the clinic with the help of friends, family, or charity.

"If [people in the northern parts of the province] haven't got the money to get there, what good is the state-of-the-art cancer clinic?"

"If there are more clinics in this province, people wouldn't have to travel or spend as much; they wouldn't be away from their families. Maybe the people on fixed incomes can't get to these clinics, so they're putting their health at risk. If there's more around the province, then the treatment is more accessible, whether it's new or not. At least they know they can go there for some kind of treatment."

"[If] the state-of-the-art [treatment clinic] is far superior than your regular limited ones [...] you might be able to go there and be cured completely."

"By presenting these things at six centres, you're diluting your money and you're diluting your quality of care too."

Preventing or treating disease

Debates about prevention versus remediation in health also triggered an impassioned,

"If you don't try to do something about [prevention] then you're doomed to have more

but split response from participants. Participants were asked to choose between funding heart disease research or expanding heart disease clinics. For many, prevention through research is the priority, but others would choose to cut down on specialized treatment in order to provide a more basic level of care to the greater number of people. For some, the issue is simple equity. For others, the sentiment seems to be that one needs to acknowledge the limitations of medical expertise and accept that *"when your time has come, you must be ready to go."*

Another trade-off focused on the life prospects of very young children. Participants were asked to choose between well-baby clinics and intensive services for critically ill infants. Again, many considered prevention more important. What many people articulated, however, were two value priorities identified above, including:

people who will get heart disease, and by the time you get around to saying, 'What about that breakthrough research?' you've got so many people in these new expanded treatment clinics that costs just keep snowballing and you're putting your money into a money pit. I think prevention is always the best answer."

"I bet you every one of us here could probably be kept alive until we're 100, if we had millions and millions of dollars. But we don't. So somewhere you've got to cut the line. You've got to draw that line. And I'm very sorry for the person that's on the other side of the line and it will be me one of these days, I know it. But you've got to do it. You get your best buck by getting everyone to live a healthier lifestyle so that when the line does come down, you're 90 years old and you've had a good life."

- offering the greatest good for the greatest number of people, and
- investment in future generations.

Participants found this an extremely difficult decision. Many participants believed that, in a time of fiscal restraint, money should go first to programs that assisted the greatest number of people. They chose to cut funding from the intensive care program because it aided only a few. Others believed that money should be used first on programs that assisted the neediest. This trade-off often sparked a discussion of income inequities and funding alternatives. Many objected to well-baby care because it meant that public resources would go to those who could pay. Some also saw a huge inequity in the fact that poor families would be disadvantaged because their critically ill children would not receive adequate care.

Public polarization on this issue was demonstrated in the two groups who voted to develop third options. One group wanted funding for both programs to be cut – they wanted families to pay for well-baby care and the voluntary sector to raise money to pay for intensive services. The second group refused to cut services for either option, on the grounds that investment in children should come before all other health priorities.

With an aging population, and with advances in medical technology, increased demands are likely to be placed on health care funding just at a time when fiscal restraint is essential. In this context, it will be increasingly important to work through these complex polarizations in order to define a solid base of values and principles for upcoming decisions.

Education

Education is among Canadians' highest priorities; almost two in three of us would rather increase taxes or the deficit than reduce spending in this area (Table 48). Only Ontarians and older Canadians are more likely to say they would rather cut spending (Table 49).

Canadians believe that, by fostering education, our institutions are investing in future generations. This investment, therefore, expresses the value of collective responsibility for young people. Group participants affirmed public support of free and universal primary and secondary education, sometimes through their silence: unlike other issues, primary and secondary education generated relatively little discussion and no controversy.

This did not imply that participants thought that the education system was perfect. In fact, many called for educational reforms.

Post-secondary education

"The more education they have the better off that the people are, not the individuals, but people in general."

"It's got to come back down to a complete overhaul and change of the education system [...] teachers that are trained differently for today's society – to go in and help the young kids [understand] how things are different now, what they can do for themselves, how they can feel better about themselves, how they can structure their whole lives to make the right decisions. So that they don't leave school and have to go on welfare."

"As one woman on disability said, 'As long as I don't go in as a full student, I can get my university education on bursaries, which is pretty good, as long as it will last. I want to go into law, so that means I am going to spend double the amount of time in school than anyone else because I can't afford to pay for it myself and I can't work'."

"I think education is the primary concern. With education, the rest will come."

Poll results and discussion groups shed different lights on the issue of collective and individual responsibility for post-secondary education. Public opinion data suggest that many Canadians support more limited accessibility. In 1994, over 2 in 3 Canadians agreed that "post-secondary education is an investment and individual Canadians should take more responsibility for paying for their own education." Despite the fact that 6 in 10 agree that the cost of university tuition is already a barrier preventing many students from attending, half the population go on to agree that "even if tuition fees were to double, students should still pay more of the cost of their education" (Table 50). This seems to suggest a belief that Canadians should not get something for nothing. However, younger Canadians and those reporting lower household incomes are more likely to express concern about access to post-secondary education.

Discussion groups' views on whether or not individuals with ability should receive support were more complex. Some considered that people with the ability to succeed in university education had a distinct advantage, in terms of their innate talents and family backgrounds. Some participants did not necessarily want to support an employment entry program for university graduates, since they thought these individuals had started out with inherent advantages, had already received a fair share of public resources, and ought to be able to demonstrate the drive and initiative to take care of themselves. Others thought that the current economic climate created barriers, even for university graduates, that might need to be bridged through public support.

Some participants focused on potential university students who have ability but who lack the means to pay. Some participants, particularly members of the agency-recruited groups, considered it important to have either lower tuition fees or larger, more easily obtainable loans to make higher education more accessible. Many of these participants had dreams of getting ahead through education.

Education is valued because it offers access to opportunities. Overall, participants saw education as a potential avenue to personal responsibility and increased independence. Even within this value system, however, Canadians appear to be struggling with a new ambivalence about the value of education in a labour market that seems to be losing vitality. New economic realities have begun to weaken optimism that education and training will fix all ills. This is evidenced in statements that suggest that the return on educational investments is diminishing, and in criticisms of training programs. Participants in groups raise questions about how educational dollars are spent, and ask how dollars can be more fairly distributed.

As the expected benefits of education are further dampened, more fundamental questions surface about the fairness of the Canadian economic system. As growing numbers of younger, educated Canadians find themselves unable to enter the labour market, and as skills translate less frequently into well-paying, secure jobs, Canadians appear more disillusioned about the breach of an implicit promise – that educational investments will pay off and that by trying harder, they will get ahead.

"The university graduates that are coming out of university right now are not getting jobs. Yes, they have the academics but they don't have any work experience that ties in with it, and it is the work experience that gets you the job as well as your credentials."

"Why should we invest in this [training] if there are not jobs out there?"

Many called for reforms to link post-secondary education to the labour force, referring to what they saw as a potential crisis for youth entering the job market. In considering a trade-off between funding an employment-entry program for post-secondary students, and care for the terminally ill, many participants chose the first alternative. Again, some participants in agency-recruited groups resisted support for university graduates, seeing them as a privileged minority that would inappropriately draw on public funds required for more needy groups.

Canadians seek to bridge these dilemmas by imagining a more integrated income security and employment system that links the social and economic agendas. The findings here suggest that education is an area where Canadians expect results for their efforts. This means that dilemmas about access, quality, relevance, and links to the labour market are likely to increase in intensity.

Other Programs

In addition to health and education programs, discussion groups worked through issues concerning Old Age Security, family allowances and, although it did not come within the purview of this study, Unemployment Insurance. These discussions helped to illuminate further Canadians' views on universality, caring, self-reliance and collective responsibility.

In public opinion polls, the data to support universality of Old Age Security is ambiguous. In 1990, two in three Canadians agreed that the old age pension should be paid to all seniors (Table 51). Consistent with this view, half of Canadians agreed in 1993 that the government should *not* provide public pensions to seniors with above-average incomes (Table 52). A year later, a majority (57%) agreed that "It's unfair to restrict our Old Age Security benefits for those who have contributed to the country throughout their lives" (Table 53). The endurance of universality in some of these responses may reflect the fact that the questions refer to targets that would eliminate rewards to those who have contributed throughout their working lives.

"You [another participant] made a statement [...] that if someone has a lot of money that maybe they can afford to pay for a service and if someone doesn't have a lot of money, they may have the service provided for them. I disagree with that because I think that if a person is motivated enough to have achieved, he should be entitled to the same rights, because of his tax dollars, as anyone who is poor [...] I don't think that there should be any penalties for the Canadians who have worked hardest."

"I wouldn't disagree with that, that there could be a cut-off point if you had an income at a certain level."

However, participants in one group used the example of Old Age Security as a program that could be targeted to save resources. Similarly, a 1994 survey showed that two in three Canadians agree that public pensions must be targeted over the long term (Table 54).

Income support for seniors and programs for individuals with a disability are among Canadians' highest priorities. More than two in three of us would rather raise taxes or increase the deficit than reduce social spending in these two areas (Table 48).

However, elder care and care for individuals with disabilities also raise paradoxes in the context of state and family reliance. Time-series data reveal that the public consensus has shifted quickly and considerably in recent years. Where just over one-third of Canadians agreed in 1989 that "many people in hospital could be looked after equally well at home," this had

"I think we lost that sense of kinship in our society. We ship them off to the old folks' home. I don't want to be a parent like that. I would like my child to be around. It would be nice to think that they take care of me some day, instead of just forgetting me."

"We're not able to do [family support] in communities the way that communities once could."

"We take care of our kids. Our kids take care of us when we get older. That's the centre that we all have to come back to. It's family."

increased to a majority by 1992, and to almost three in four Canadians by 1994 (Table 55). These results suggest that over time, and undoubtedly fuelled by considerable public debate, Canadians have moved away from institutional solutions to a new or resumed reliance on the family.

On this issue, Canadians recognize that increased responsibility must be accompanied by increased support. For example, in 1994, there was a high level of agreement with support payments to families who care for an elderly family member (Table 56). In fact, 7 in 10 Canadians said they would be willing to pay additional taxes to support these elder-care payments. Support is highest among those with lower income, but men and women do not differ.

Some group participants also saw elder care at home as an area that requires state support. Perhaps because these responsibilities fall when many women have joined the labour market, or perhaps because they mean bringing a previously independent person back into the home, discussants often recognized that it is crucial to complement family supports with broader state and community supports.

In discussions, care of individuals with disabilities is even more likely to be viewed as a collective responsibility. Compassion is high for these fellow citizens. These individuals are seen as "deserving" income and other kinds of supports by virtue of being placed at an unfair disadvantage through no fault of their own. Only rarely did discussants suggest that families should shoulder these responsibilities alone.

"People have disabilities, only so much energy, and don't have access to resources. I can do my share, but I need the government to do their share of listening to me as well."

"Somewhere, somebody could get mad and cut strings along the line and I could get in an uncomfortable situation [...] That's why us little people don't speak up sometimes. We're scared we'll lose what we have."

In contrast, Canadians' support for universal family allowances has weakened over time. In the mid-1980s, the public was divided over the application of means tests "for social programs such as family allowance" (Table 57). By 1989, using a differently worded question, half of those picked supported family allowances going only to the needy (Table 58). By 1990, and again with different wording, a majority supported family allowances being paid only to low-income families (Table 59).

Canadians are also more willing to consider reshaping Unemployment Insurance benefits according to need and targeting the program according to patterns of use. Polling data show that two-thirds of Canadians support lower benefits for frequent UI users (Table 60). Moreover, many Canadians support the idea that beneficiaries should be required to take training programs. They are, however, less decided on whether UI benefits should be based on household, as opposed to personal, income, or whether people who experience more frequent periods of unemployment should pay higher premiums (Table 61).

None of the discussion-group trade-offs raised the topic of Unemployment Insurance, since the groups' focus was on programs affected by the proposed Canada Health and Social Transfer. However, participants favoured integrating program benefits in their discussions of training options for people returning to the labour force.

Working through these issues to formulate informed public judgment and refine this new principle in a changed social and economic climate will take time. Canadians are just coming to terms with the wider social and economic context of the demands placed on the income security system.

4. Canadians' Vision for Canada

In their opening statements about what they most valued about living in Canada, discussion group participants frequently mentioned the freedoms, rights, and opportunities that the country offers. Most participants said they believe that Canada is and should be a land of opportunity. They also valued the country's freedom of speech and choice.

Should the Majority Rule?

In 1993, Canadians who were asked to choose between two opposing democratic principles – majority rule and minority protection – chose majority rule by a two-to-one margin (Table 62). Similarly, in discussion groups, most participants believe that in the Canadian democracy, the majority should rule, while the minority has the opportunity to sway majority opinion. A few participants wanted consensus to be used as a first resort, where practical. Canadians envision a dynamic system in which minorities play an important corrective role. Consistent with their concerns about adequate democratic engagement, they also reject the notion that minorities should simply "fit in." The rights of minorities should not be "trampled" just because they don't dominate.

Participants pointed out that some minorities, including the powerful, the wealthy, and special interest and lobby groups, have power over the majority. The real issue for some was that the "silent majority" was not heard. At the same time, other participants expressed concern that less powerful minorities could experience discrimination.

"The majority has to listen to what the minority has to say, because some day that minority is going to be the majority. The tables are going to turn somewhere down the line. They just can't afford to completely ignore the minority."

"Their job is to create an opposition, to voice their opinion [...]."

"It might be true that the majority rules for policy and procedures, but I don't think that under any circumstance do minorities of any sort – whether they be political, religious, racial – have to fit with anybody [...] you have the right to decide whether or not you want to be a part of something."

"I feel that the majority rule is the easy way out. It's a way to get things done quickly, to push things through, but the aftermath is much more lengthy and much more complicated than if people understand and a consensus is reached [...]. And I believe that all that is, is educating each other and working it out. So yes, it may be more difficult to arrive at a consensus in the beginning. But in the long run, it's much more efficient and better for everyone."

Regional Equity

In a 1988 survey, Canadians indicated that they believe that regional disparities should not be accepted as a normal result of market forces. In their minds, intervention is needed to assist regional development. In 1994, 7 in 10 Canadians believed that the federal government should give incentives for firms to create jobs in the poorer regions of Canada (Table 63).

In polls, equity across provinces and regions is strongly supported by Canadians. Discussion group participants in the West and East referred more often than those in central Canada to regional equity. While some participants voiced reservations about efforts to seek regional equity, they felt a sense of collective responsibility for the well-being of individuals in other provinces. Others identified the need to reduce barriers between provinces, including trade, attitudes, and approaches.

"It drives me crazy because I live in one of the most wonderful provinces and yet my province is suffering behind, as well as the rest of the Maritimes. I think that answers to the fact that our political system just isn't working towards Canada as a whole. It has to be more regionalized."

"There are groups that need attention in the Maritimes. I think Ontario and Quebec get more than their fair share of things. Their wealth over the generations has come at our expense because that's where the population is."

Participants did not hold fixed views about how regional equity could best be achieved. For some it was a sharing of federal tax dollars and a federal responsibility, but others made it clear that the provinces themselves had a responsibility to work together in the interest of all Canadians.

Gallup Canada tracking research between 1988 and 1990 showed strong support for regional transfers to the "have-not" provinces (Table 64). Over this period, a steady 6 in 10 Canadians wanted the federal government to increase spending on poorer regions, a level of support for increased spending as high as that for education and health. It also appears that support for regional equity measures have increased slightly over time. In 1990, only 1 in 10 Canadians suggested that government spending on poorer regions should be decreased or eliminated. A similarly small number of Canadians "disapproved" of regional transfers back in 1972 (Table 65).

Another potential form of regional assistance, assisting unemployed people in "have not" regions to find work or relocate, is not as well received. In polls, Canadians appear to believe that people should not have to leave their communities to find work and that efforts should be directed at creating jobs in poorer regions. While the population is divided on this issue, few believed the federal government should not be involved in the issue of the special needs of the unemployed in poorer regions (Table 66). Among those who believed the federal government should be involved, more tend to support the idea of providing financial assistance to those who wish to stay home.

In discussions, participants were most often divided on the issue of leaving their homes and communities to find work. Many felt that people no longer have a choice, but they were concerned about how the loss of family and other supports could further compound problems. At the same time, a few expressed concern that people could be leaving with false hopes and that job opportunities might not be better elsewhere. This concern stemmed from the stiff competition for jobs, compounded by the threat of added competition from newcomers from out of province. It also related to concerns expressed about the influx of immigrants to already tight labour markets.

In terms of mechanisms to address regional equity in incomes and services, as data presented in Chapter 1 suggest, in 1994, almost 7 in 10 Canadians believed that the federal government had a role to play to "redistribute wealth in order to maintain social equality" (Table 19). More importantly, in July/August 1995, 60% of Canadians agreed that Canadians have a right to expect a minimum level of service wherever they live, including 66% of Albertans but only 48% of Quebecers. Only 36% felt that provinces are best able to decide what services are needed, with most residents in most provinces agreeing only about 32% of the time, and Quebecers agreeing 49% of the time (Table 20).

As stated above, the view of national standards varies across health, education, and income support. In July/August 1995, 94% of Canadians saw standards as essential in health care (80% as very essential), 88% as essential in university/college education (56% as very essential), and 78% as essential in social assistance (but only 36% as very essential). Respectively, only 2, 4, and 6% said that standards were not at all essential (Table 21).

Canadians, however, are undecided about the best way to develop national standards: 54% agree that, failing an agreement with the provinces, the federal government should establish the standards itself and withhold money from provinces that do not meet those standards. Strikingly, those in Atlantic Canada are most in agreement at 70% (Table 22).

National standards are clearly important to achieving regional equity in the minds of Canadians. However, they feel uncertain about how to achieve these. Participants addressing these issues did not have a clear picture of jurisdictional issues. While asking that the provinces start working together, they still need to work through the role of the federal government. Canadians in discussions are more likely to address content of social programs, not issues surrounding the machinery of government.

Immigration

Immigration and immigration levels have long been a contentious issue in Canadian society. Research over the last few years indicates that approximately half the population believes too many immigrants are being admitted to Canada (Table 67), opposition that may well be linked to concerns regarding employment. In 1989, during the last phase of the boom years, only one in three Canadians supported a decrease in immigration levels (Table 68). By 1994, with far higher unemployment rates, half supported a decrease. Research in 1994 may have revealed the reason for this fluctuation when it showed that only one in three Canadians believe that "immigrants create more jobs than they take away" from Canadians (Table 69).

There is also a growing concern about the composition of the new immigrant population. Between 1993 and 1994, the belief that Canada's immigration policy allows too many people of different races and cultures into Canada increased very slightly (Table 70), a change that might be a result of sampling error. To the extent this is a real trend, however, it may be fuelled by concerns that new immigrants do not share the same principles and values: one in three Canadians believed this to be the case (Table 69). This may also be further evidence of the specific version of multiculturalism that Canadians endorse.

While immigration was not raised in a trade-off decision, individuals in some groups mentioned it in their introductory statements as one of the things they would most like to change about Canada. What some participants considered to be the country's counter-productive immigration policy also arose as an issue as participants struggled with problems related to employment and competition. While most were not opposed to immigration per se, they thought the sole reason for the country's immigration policy should be to provide net economic benefit. Their impression of the current system was that too many immigrants were ill-equipped to function in Canadian society and so ended up relying on the state, a situation unfair to the Canadian taxpayer and to citizens in need of social assistance. They found it difficult to understand why, if the country had a shortage of jobs, the government was allowing more people to enter the country and compete against those already here. Some participants were concerned about immigrants taking low paying jobs and keeping the minimum wage down. Only a tiny minority of participants who discussed this issue believed that Canada should increase immigration levels.

Canadians envision a multicultural society that respects and accepts diversity, but they also expect immigrants to adopt the values of other Canadians. Proud of their multicultural heritage, most agreed in 1994 that "a mixture of different lifestyles and cultures makes Canada a more attractive place to live" (Table 71). More agreed that "one of the best sources of our Canadian identity is that fact that we are a nation of immigrants," than agreed that "the traditional Canadian way of life is being threatened by high levels of immigration." Relatively few Canadians want to "turn the clock back."

Diversity and Equity

Multiculturalism is seen as enriching Canadian culture, and this view is increasing over time (Tables 72 and 73). There is overwhelming support for the notion of a society where different races and cultures live and work together so that they can better understand each other (Table 74).

The polling data suggests, however, that there are different understandings of multiculturalism. Canadians in 1995 largely rejected the notion of a society where members of the community share the same language, race and religion (Table 75). On the other end of the continuum, Canadians also reject a society where members follow a way of life particular to their religion or race. Instead, three in four Canadians describe their "ideal" society as one that is multicultural, but where members share "a common way of life and common values." Where there is a conflict between minority traditions and this "way of life," there is a high level of agreement that the majority should take precedence (Tables 76 and 77).

Indeed, tracking research between 1993 and 1995 shows that the proportion who believe that "different ethnic groups should try to adapt to the value system and way of life of the majority in Canadian society" may have increased slightly (Table 78). This supports 1987 data indicating that most Canadians also believed that immigrants should try harder to be like "other Canadians," and to "learn what it is to be Canadian [rather] than cling to their old ways" (Tables 79 and 80).

These views were echoed by discussion group participants. Some said that one of the things they most valued about living in Canada was its multicultural nature and tolerant attitudes. Others worried that the focus on individual cultures was detrimental to Canada as a whole. It appeared that participants were willing to tolerate Canadian diversity and are often proud of it, as long as their vision of the "Canadian way of life" and "Canadian family values" is not jeopardized. Further engagement with Canadians may tap into deeper ambivalence on this critical issue.

As a new generation of Canadians raised in a multicultural milieu grows up, a greater openness to diversity may be developing. Where a small majority (56%) agreed in 1974 that "People coming to the country should change their behaviour to be more like Canadians," those agreeing had declined to 46% in 1991 (Table 81). More dialogue is needed to understand what it is that Canadians want others to change – values or incidental behaviour.

Canadians limit the roles they see for the federal government in encouraging multiculturalism. Almost 9 in 10 Canadians rejected an increase in spending on multiculturalism groups, with equal proportions saying spending should remain at current levels or saying it should be decreased (Table 82). While in 1974, 7 in 10 Canadians had agreed that government should support activities aimed at preserving cultural heritages, less than 6 in 10 agreed with this support in 1991 (Table 71). This data must be viewed with caution, however, given slightly different wording and ordering of the questions. In 1995, just over half of those polled supported "the federal government's current multiculturalism policy" (Table 83).

This wish for a curtailed federal role is also evident in the elements of federal multiculturalism that garner the most support (Table 84). Ensuring rights and equality through measures aimed at integration, non-discrimination, and cultural tolerance and re-

"We all deserve to have equal treatment, but if somebody's had a wrongdoing towards them, they should be compensated for it [...] Japanese Canadians during the war, First Nations people [...]."

spect receive the highest levels of support. Measures aimed at actively promoting differences are rejected by the majority (Table 85).

Tolerance

Canada's self-image is that of a nation with a great deal of tolerance for people from different ethnic or religious groups. While polling data suggests that Canadians realize they have not reached that ideal, tracking studies suggest that over time there appears to be greater acceptance of immigrants and ethnic groups.

In 1987, 7 in 10 Canadians believed that the attitudes and beliefs of immigrants often invite intolerance (Table 86). The belief that immigrants "bring discrimination on themselves" may be indicative of a more subtle and more pervasive form of intolerance. Four in 10 Canadians agreed with the statement: "If minority groups hope to be liked better, they should try first to get rid of their harmful and irritating faults" (Table 87). This clearly demonstrated a level of intolerance. One third of Canadians also agreed that "the trouble with letting certain minority groups into a nice neighbourhood is that they gradually give it their own atmosphere" (Table 88). This latter attitude, however, may be more tied to a kind of conservatism about change in general than specifically to intolerance.

Canadians continue to grapple with the value conflicts inherent in this area of public policy and opinions, therefore, are unfixed, flexible, and open to public debate. For example, with respect to hate literature, although three-quarters agreed in 1987 that it should be against the law, close to half were willing to change their position if banning hate literature meant "less freedom of speech" (Table 89). On the other side, among those who opposed bans, 40% were willing to change their views if a non-ban were to result in "more prejudice."

In 1987, Canadians rejected the idea that there is some "natural" superiority of certain races or groups of people or that some people are "better" than others (Tables 90, 91 and 92). However, in both 1987 and 1993, they agreed that, even if all were treated equally "some people will turn out better than others" (Table 93). In valuing equality for all, they nonetheless recognized that individuals differ in talent, ability, and drive. To this end, the majority believed that, in a fair economic system, those with more ability should earn more (Table 94) and that success is "proof" of hard work (Table 95). In 1993, more than 6 in 10 Canadians agreed that "if people work hard they almost always get what they want" (Table 96).

The underlying recognition that people differ in terms of talents, ability, drive, culture, and formative experiences led some discussion group participants to consider carefully how to balance equality of opportunity and equality of treatment. In the preliminary questionnaire, a number of participants called for more rights for various groups as one of the things they would want to change about Canada.

Two studies measuring perceived racism, conducted in 1993 and 1995, found that over 8 in 10 Canadians believed that there is at least "some" racism in Canada, and a quarter of the population believed that there is a "great deal" of racism (Table 97). Further, almost three in four Canadians believed racism is a "somewhat" serious problem in Canada (Table 98).

Equal opportunity

An equal opportunity approach to public policy and hiring holds the greatest resonance for Canadians. In 1987, two in three Canadians agreed that "If people were treated more equally in this country, we would have fewer problems" (Table 99). Canadians were also quite strongly opposed to anything that

"People are not all the same. We're all very different. We have some things that make us similar in various ways, but there are a lot of people that are very different, and I don't see why we should expect to be treated the same, because we aren't."

may be interpreted as discriminatory. Three in four members of the elites and members of the general public believed that it should be against the law to write or speak in a way that promotes hatred toward a particular racial or religious group (Table 89).

Canadians also seem less inclined to believe that measures to promote equal rights are appropriate. While almost 7 in 10 *disagreed* that "We have gone too far in pushing equal rights in this country" in 1987 (Table 100), by 1993 only half of Canadians disagreed. Where a small majority (56%) of Canadians agreed in 1987 that we do *not* give everyone an equal chance in Canada, by 1993 only 4 in 10 agreed (Table 101).

While Canadians subscribe to the philosophy of equal opportunity, they also believe that the merit principle should prevail. This is often at odds with the notion of equality measures that focus on results rather than on creating a "level playing field." An equal-outcome approach, as implied by job quotas, is therefore more contentious. Although virtually all Canadians agreed in 1987 that it is important to guarantee equality between men and women in all aspects of life (Table 102), only 1 in 3 Canadians agreed that companies should have quotas to ensure that a fixed percentage of women are hired (Table 103). And 2 in 3 of those who favoured quotas said they would change their position if this meant that the best person were not hired for the job (Table 103). Alternatively, of the 2 in 3 Canadians who opposed quotas, close to half said they would feel differently about this if it meant that women were to "remain economically unequal." By 1993 the level of support for quotas had dropped to less than 1 in 10 (Table 104).

Attitudes toward job quotas are driven by a concern that merit be rewarded and "reverse discrimination" be avoided. Just over half of Canadians believed in 1991 that whites are, in fact, discriminated against in Canadian society (Table 105). Resistance to quotas is not driven by a belief that hiring is the purview of individual employers; Canadians are fully open to the notion that individual employers have a responsibility to society (Table 105).

These issues raised many controversies in discussion groups that dealt with equity statements, some of which participants were unable to work through in a single discussion. Initially some felt strongly that it was wrong that some groups received special attention, and that groups of different cultural backgrounds, such as First Nations' people and members of employment equity groups, should receive no accommodation. Others disagreed and felt that everyone should be treated individually according to his or her needs. With further discussion, most participants clarified that they believed that most groups in most situations should be treated equally, but that groups in special situations deserved different treatment.

5. The View on Partnerships

The need for new partnerships between sectors to address broad social and economic issues is a common theme for Canadians. In evoking a vision of partnership across sectors, discussion group participants wanted to contain the threat embodied in particular institutional agendas and to balance competing interests. They appeared to see different sectors as making different kinds of contributions and playing different kinds of roles in creating partnerships: charitable organizations were seen as moral leaders helping to define needs and objectives; government was seen as the appropriate sector to define rules and monitor delivery; the private sector was seen as the one to help ensure cost-effectiveness.

On the whole, participants shared a vague and idealistic sense of the potential of partnerships. They spoke about them in glowing but abstract terms. They had a few notable concerns about partnerships, however, including a fear that "partnerships could fall through" and leave "needy" individuals without any backup. One group, considering the possibility that some partnerships might be very successful and others less so, identified keys to successful partnerships, including tight agreements between the cooperating agencies.

Participants also sometimes discussed the value of partnerships' ability to adapt to local circumstances. Different kinds of partnerships were seen as appropriate to different communities, an individualization that could help ensure flexibility and sustainability.

Charitable Sector Partnerships

In polls, Canadians have recognized that the charitable sector makes a positive contribution to the community (Table 106). Most Canadians, though, see this as a "somewhat" rather than "very" positive contribution. This may be because most Canadians do not see tangible evidence of significant charitable activity and have limited exposure. When government, the charitable sector, and business are compared in terms of who would be most effective in providing a service, the charitable sector is invariably rated highest (data not shown).

"If you were to take the taxpayers' money and give it to the government and then have the government give it back to the taxpayers, you're just creating a middle-man that's going to take their share of that money. So if you eliminated that part of it, then the people could afford to have their own social programs at a lot less expense and probably a lot more volunteer work."

"With the crunch on the middle-class working person now, I know that my charitable pocket has become very thin in the past few years."

In 1987, Canadians did not see individual charitable donations as a substitute for government provision of services (Table 107), and Canadians generally believed that "the work that charitable and non-profit organizations do should not be a substitute for government's responsibility to provide services."

"I would rather have my income tax reduced [...] and [pay] a community of citizens who aren't biased, who aren't motivated by greed, who aren't selfish, who aren't racist. I think that welfare should be public."

In 1994, Canadians strongly agreed that "one of the best things about Canada and Canadians is that we are generous and prepared to help people in need" (Table 108). Indeed, individual Canadians perceived the general public in 1987 as having the greatest responsibility for providing funds to the charitable sector (Table 109). Canadians also tended to disagree with the proposition that Americans are more generous than Canadians (Table 110). The majority believed that Canadians collectively are generous (Table 111).

In fact, donation levels are generally low, with median donation levels in the region of $50 during the late 1980s. This is well below the levels achieved by individual Americans. However, fully one in four Canadians said in 1987 that it was "very" likely they would volunteer their time to a charity or non-profit organization if asked (Table 112).

The most common reason given by individuals who said they had not donated was that they simply could not afford it (Table 113). There was a high level of disagreement with the proposition that one should "give until it hurts" (Table 110). There was only a small agreement that the amount of money donated by Canadians to non-profit organizations be doubled (Table 112).

Eight in 10 agreed in 1994 that high taxes are reducing Canadians' compassion for those in need (Table 114). It may be that Canadians believe that assisting those in need is a community or government responsibility rather than one to be shouldered by the individual, but the paradox is that governments cannot assist those in need without the contributions of individual taxpayers. The duality between individualism and collectivism, noted above, translates into a belief that the state exists to help those in need. This, in turn, may lead to a more limited sense of personal responsibility for others.

Canadian priorities for the charitable sector closely reflected their priorities for government and public policy in 1987 (Table 115): health care, assistance to the disadvantaged, and education were all high priorities, as was protection of the environment; arts, culture, and Third World development were lower priorities.

In discussions groups, the priorities were similar. Members of some randomly recruited groups said that charities should take over much of the delivery of the services to the "needy." There was a feeling that the government, as the middle party between taxpayers and service recipients, was poorly administered and charitable organizations were seen as a preferable middle party.

For the most part, the participants who dealt with the trade-off on partnership seemed to believe that people will support charities, but not that charities should take over. Only on a few occasions did participants go so far as to suggest that charitable sector involvement might fully replace government's current role. Questions also arose about whether charities, with financial donations from the public and volunteers, would be able to fulfil the need. Some participants believed that charitable organizations might have difficultly stepping into the breach of government cuts. People rarely brought up how much time or money they might personally be willing to give to charitable organizations, or whether they would be willing to pay more taxes to support the charitable sector.

Views of the value and feasibility of charitable sector involvement have not been closely worked through by Canadians and this discussion remains at an abstract level. While confidence in the charitable sector appears to be high, Canadians are uncertain about the load that the charitable sector may be able to bear, and about whether or not it is an appropriate sector to take on responsibility for social programs. Most Canadians, in polls and discussion groups, appear to think that the charitable sector should be a partner, but not a substitute for government in the domain of social programs.

Private Sector Partnerships

In the early 1990s, Canadians endorsed the principle of private sector involvement in providing public services and considered that sector to have a certain responsibility (Tables 116 and 117). However, the polling data also suggest that Canadians had doubts about the sector's role in concrete scenarios. For example, in the area of social programs such as pensions and child care, only one in five believed that responsibility should be shifted to the private sector (Table 118) and only one in three described the private sector's responsibility to the poor as "major" (Table 117).

"No drug company is going to make any money off me living a better lifestyle. That's why that kind of research has to be funded because the research for asthma and even heart drugs, the companies will do that because they are going to make some money off it. That kind of research you can't make money off."

"I think it's time that big business gets a little bit more involved with feeding the hungry folk."

Canadians continue to adhere to the security of the public sector providing services and, at most, see the private sector as a potential partner with the public sector. Total transfer of responsibility, however, is approached with caution. Canadians see the private sector as a potential service deliverer with government playing an important role in establishing and monitoring rules for that involvement.

This is, perhaps, not surprising given a fairly high level of distrust of the private sector (Tables 119 and 120). In 1985, over 4 in 10 agreed that corporations operating in Canada "make too much money," and the proportion saying this had increased slightly from earlier in the decade. As well, more Canadians in 1993 accepted the proposition that "under the free enterprise system, working people do not get their fair share of what they produce," than believed that "when businesses are allowed to make as much money as they can, everyone profits in the long run, including the poor."

Unlike trust in government, however, trust in the private sector may have strengthened over time. In January 1983, half agreed that "the free market system is working worse than it used to." By July 1985, the proportion saying this had decreased to just under a quarter (Table 121).

In the discussion groups, many randomly recruited participants also supported greater involvement of the private/for-profit sector in areas traditionally handled by government. However, participants felt that caution should be exercised in devolving responsibilities. There was concern that "big business" would ultimately be concerned with the "bottom line" and perhaps could not be trusted to deliver compassionate services on their own. Sometimes this was expressed as a conflict of interest that would rule out private sector involvement. At other times, it was expressed as a question of allowing privatization, but ensuring that rules would be in place to maintain access and quality.

"People, individuals, charitable organizations, businesses are stepping in and taking some control over helping people instead of stepping back and saying 'the government should do that.' That is a very positive thing."

"Non-profit organizations could benefit from big business and big business could use a little bit of humbling from non-profit and it's taking the two resources necessary to make a program work and getting them together. I like the idea of government being the facilitator or catalyst."

6. Government and Engagement

Government remains a favourite target of criticism for Canadians, but perception of governments' influence varies by issue area. Only one in four agreed in 1993 that "governments cannot do much to solve our economic problems" (Table 122). Indeed, in the area of the economy and the environment, a 1994 survey found that most Canadians believe the federal government can have a relatively high degree of influence (Table 123). And among a number of issue statements, Canadians were least likely to agree with the negative statement "I don't think the federal government can really influence our economic future" (Table 124). Similarly, few agreed with the negative view that "it's hard to believe government can really make a difference" with respect to social problems including violence, poverty and disease (Table 124).

In 1987, 8 in 10 Canadians agreed that "too many people want someone else to help them solve their problems instead of solving them themselves" (Table 125). This does not, however, seem to mean a reduced role for government. In 1994 (Table 19) most Canadians approved of government's role across a broad range of activities, including:

	% approval
Protecting citizens from crime and abuse	87
Ensuring jobs for those willing and able to work	85
Planning for the future	83
Developing partnerships	82
Ensuring the highest possible standard of living and quality of life	80

More than three in four Canadians also considered that government should have a role in promoting tolerance and understanding and ensuring a fair and efficient marketplace. While most accept a wide range of roles for government, Canadians are not inclined to see government as a "positive force" in their own lives (Table 126).

Waste and Inefficiency

One of the more visible root causes of the public disaffection with government is waste and inefficiency. Responses to a 1993 question on this issue clearly indicate the depth of public concern (Table127): 8 in 10 Canadians indicated that they believe "people in government ... waste a lot of the money we pay in taxes"; this is a significant increase over 1988. Virtually the same result was found in a 1994 survey question, which proposed that, "the real problem with the federal government is the waste and inefficiency of the bureaucracy" (Table 128). Over 8 in 10 Canadians agreed with this statement.

While many surveys over the years have explored the issue of federal government waste and inefficiency, Gallup Poll data also reveals that all three levels of government are thought to be wasteful (Table 129). In 1988, participants were asked how many cents of every tax dollar are wasted by their municipal, provincial and federal governments. The highest dollar value estimate of wastage was for the federal government, followed closely by the provincial governments. Municipalities were well behind and are clearly considered to be the most efficient with taxpayer money.

While Canadians are concerned about deficit reduction, they are also unwilling to accept program cuts. In 1994, close to half of the Canadians polled believed that waste and inefficiency were contributing to our public debt, and that if efficiency could be improved and waste eliminated, the deficit could be reduced and programs maintained (Table 130).

Discussion group participants differed in their acceptance of funding cuts. Members of randomly recruited groups appeared to be more willing to accept cost reduction and were very concerned with getting Canada's house in order by tightening up government waste and reducing abuse of social assistance. Members of agency-recruited groups felt that cuts to welfare were inappropriate targets for government cutbacks. They felt that decision makers should be required to share citizens' experiences before judging them or changing policies that would have major impacts on their lives. All groups were afraid that the social safety net could be eroded beyond repair if cuts were not made thoughtfully and strategically.

"My major value is I don't think the government should be so goddam top heavy. Get rid of the management. Shrink the management down and put the people where you need them. For one, they don't get paid as much so you can fire two [managers] and you can hire three other people."

"We don't need all those Senators. What is there, 200 or something like that? That's ridiculous. What a waste of money."

In the area of medical services, 8 in 10 Canadians agreed that "cuts to medical services could be completely avoided if the health care system were just made more efficient" (Table 131) and if waste were eliminated (Table 132). Canadians had explicit criticisms of, and suggestions relating to, waste and inefficiency in the health care system. A majority believed that:

- doctors are prescribing unnecessarily,
- patients are using health services they do not need,
- patients are being looked after in a hospital when they could be treated as well in their homes, and
- hospitals are not managing their finances economically.

Moreover, this perception of waste has been increasing steadily over time.

Many Canadians believe that greater effectiveness and efficiency in program delivery could go a long way to ensuring that tax dollars are better spent. In the late 1980s, for example, more described the government's performance in helping the needy as "poor" than "good" (Table 133). This belief has increased over time, parallelling a growing cynicism with governance and the capabilities of our leaders.

"There isn't any department of government that knows what their job is because you talk to five different people in the same department and you get five different stories and none of them has a clue about what the other person was talking about. Or it's not their job."

A few discussion group participants, mostly members of the agency-recruited groups, had complaints about front-line government employees. Disrespect, inconsistent behaviour, and limited knowledge on the part of the people administering government programs only increased the frustration with programs. The sense here seemed to be not only that programs may be poorly designed and organized, but that they are managed in ways that work against rather than with recipients. Many participants in contact with government services complained that they had to go through a maze of people and paperwork just to find out what programs were available and how they worked. In their eyes, these inefficiencies wasted time and effort on all sides, but also have clear impacts on the ability of programs to make a difference.

Participants in every discussion group expressed their frustration at the waste they perceived in political conduct and government operations. Administrative efficiency was often mentioned as one of the things they would most like the government to achieve. Participants indicated that savings could be achieved by dealing with abuse of the welfare system and inefficiencies in health care, to maintain affordable services. Many participants also damned the "exorbitant" salaries and benefits of politicians and government officials as clear examples of waste and rejected other types of government expenditure as wasteful.

"I feel strongly that they are really, really extracting a lot of money out of the middle class that really shouldn't be coming out that way, and then part of the problem is because the darn thing is just too big. We somehow are forgetting that the original concept is that the money that I make is mine. Then, yes, I am going to share it, but it is mine first."

"I think they are overpaid because after they do their term – say at the municipal level they do a three- to four-year term – they get a lump sum cash settlement saying, 'Thanks for coming out.' Why can't they just go out and be like another unemployed citizen?"

Participants were less clear about who is responsible for what. They did not pin responsibility on one level of government as opposed to another, but worked on the assumption that affordability is a concern across the country and should be a shared burden. These findings suggest that social programs must be affordable and fiscally responsible and that they must be based on acceptable levels of taxation and adequate transfer arrangements. As seen above in the section on the role of government, and on regional equity, Canadians are struggling to redefine responsibilities and want more information to inform the process of working through these issues.

When asked what they would most like to change about living in Canada, participants often mentioned what they believed to be unfair taxation. No one expressed willingness to pay more taxes for future benefit, but pointed instead to low corporate tax rates and "misleading hype" about the deficit. Many participants expressed concerns about the level of taxation and called for a restructuring of the tax system.

Canadians weigh cost-effectiveness carefully when trading off options for social policy reform. Discussion group participants sent a clear message that cost alone should not be the sole criteria for deciding on the program worthiness. When discussing priority trade-offs, participants raised major concerns about ineffective program structures, a lack of incentives and a lack of coordination between training and labour force demands, caused partly, they believed, by poorly defined objectives and government ineptitude. They wanted to support effective programs that are tailored to solve the problems at hand, not just cut for the sake of cuts.

A substantial proportion of the population suggested that social programs need to be overhauled, and that simply cleaning up waste and abuse will not go far enough (Table 130). This suggests that Canadians see other problems besides inefficiency.

Trust in Government

Public opinion poll data and qualitative findings reveal high levels of distrust of elected officials and bureaucracy, with little distinction made between politicians and paid government employees, or among different political parties.

The growing disillusionment with government reflects a generalized malaise directed at large institutions. While less pronounced, the media, business, religion, and the justice system also suffer from a lack of public confidence. There is little doubt, however, that federal and provincial governments enjoy the lowest levels of trust (Table 134). Big business receives slightly lesser levels of mistrust. Municipal governments are sometimes seen as slightly more in touch, and therefore more trustworthy.

Public opinion poll data suggests that this lack of trust in government is primarily directed at its agents rather than the system itself. In polls few Canadians believe that, inherently, government "threatens the rights of people and must not be trusted" (Table 135). Polls suggest that Canadians believe, however, that the ethical standards of politicians and government have slipped in recent years (Table 136). In the late 1980s and early 1990s, close to half agreed that "quite a few of the people running the government are a little crooked," (Table 137) and a small majority of Canadians agreed that politicians cannot be trusted to tell the truth or to do what is best for the country (Table 138).

"I used to believe that if I just had ten minutes with him, I could tell him what he's doing to affect people. And I've realized that it wouldn't matter if I had ten days with him, one on one. It's not going to matter. He really doesn't care. It doesn't matter how much information he has when it comes down to his values."

"The level of government closest to your community ... tends more to stay within the guidelines of doing what they said they would do because they will be held accountable on a personal basis. You have their phone number and you know where they live. Higher levels of government, you don't have that accessibility

Canadians also question the competence of our leaders and public service. Two in three Canadians believed that the federal government knows what it is doing "only some of the time," and this concern increased appreciably in the early 1990s, compared to the late 1980s (Table 139). When asked in 1994, only 1 in 3 Canadians trusted the government to make the appropriate changes to social programs (Table 140). The general public also feels "divorced" from its leaders who, they believe, exhibit arrogance and symptoms of isolation. Eight in 10 agree that those elected to Parliament tend to lose touch with the people (Table 141). Three in 4 say "I don't think the government cares much what people like me think."

to them and I don't think they feel that responsibility to the people they were put in place to act for."

"He was the honest Joe that was going to help everybody but the corruption got him when he got in there."

Participants in discussion groups debated whether politicians lose touch with the public, were ever in touch, or simply do not care. Politicians were accused of making promises to get elected and then not carrying them out once they are in office. Participants also discussed the corrupting influence of power itself and the tendency for a politician to promote his or her "own agenda" and build an empire.

Many participants blamed the size, internal hierarchy, and monolithic structure of government for its ills. Others commented on the threat posed by ties across big institutions. They felt that the government makes decisions based on what the powerful and wealthy want, not the average person's needs.

Nevertheless, as participants began to consider the problem more deeply, they acknowledged the difficulty of meeting everyone's wants and needs and began to take more responsibility for their own actions, to resist passivity, and to look for new solutions. Those with personal stories of government inefficiency expressed the most frustration in being heard, but many others also felt powerless to act.

Democratic Engagement

Canadians' belief in the basic tenets of democracy is increasingly qualified by unrest about whether our democratic institutions are living up to their mandates. In struggling to define a more responsive process, Canadians also wrestle with the age-old problem of democratic engagement. They seem well aware that democratic institutions require more information, participation, and commitment. Uncertainty and frustration prevail, however, about how best to achieve these in the Canadian context.

Significant majorities of the general public believe that most Canadians are capable of public judgment, and that the grass roots are a good source of solutions to difficult problems facing government. A government that is

"With freedom comes responsibility. So any time you have freedom, you have a big responsibility, not only to each other but to yourself. And that's sometimes a very hard thing to control."

elected and representative is also strongly supported, with only 1 in 25 in 1993 suggesting
our society would be better if Canada stopped
having elections (Table 142). Echoing wide-
spread cynicism and mistrust in elected officials, however, only 1 in 3 Canadians believe that life
in Canada would be "much worse" if elections were abolished.

"I enjoy freedom, responsible freedom, the ability to do what you want. But you have to have responsibility for your actions."

Discussion group participants' complex
and often vehement views provide a rich, de-
spairing picture of Canadians' relationship to
governance. As group participants worked
through these issues, they offered important
clues about how to make government more
responsive and trustworthy. They want more
engagement, information, transparency, and
flexibility from government. 1993 polling data
also expresses a desire for involvement and
transparency in governance (Table 143). The
vast majority of Canadians (85%) agree that
"in a democracy, no political decisions should
be made in secret."

"Politicians try to be all things to all people and they can't be. You can't please everybody. You have to show leadership and say, 'This is what the people put us in to do' and carry on."

"We're talking about government here as if it's the devil. But actually, the people are the government, and all of a sudden we're saying we're all against this government. But yet, we got this government elected."

"I would like people to realize that government is not us and them, that people elect the government and the only way things can change is we all become more involved."

Democracy and freedom are crucial for
discussion group participants. In a question-
naire response to an open-ended item about the thing they most valued about living in Canada,
freedom and democracy taken together ranked highest: 63% of agency participants and 69% of
randomly recruited participants mentioned freedom and/or democracy.

In discussions, participants pointed to free
speech and the opportunity to exercise one's
vote to change the government as central values. As participants considered trade-offs and
options, they often began to see their own contributions as increasingly crucial. To restore
trust and relevance, participants in many
groups discussed new ways to generate decisions, including the participation of commit-
tees of "ordinary" Canadians from different
backgrounds.

"It should be law that he has to follow that campaign as best he can, instead of saying, 'I'm going to lower taxes and I'm going to do this and I'm going to do that,' and do nothing in office and just sit there and smile."

"I think party solidarity has a lot to do with what the new guy can achieve. I mean, he gets in there with all kinds of good ideas and he's probably in touch with the people. But, you know, there's half a dozen people at the top of the party who run the party, and then elected members vote the way they're told. If they don't, you see what happens to them."

Paradoxically, in 1993 close to half of the
Canadian population agreed that "the government should pay the most attention to those
citizens who are well informed" (Table 143).
Similarly, close to half agreed that "the problem

with democracy is that most people don't really know what's best for them." These responses may suggest an elitist perspective among Canadians answering polls. Canadians also agreed that it is necessary to have a small group of people who really run things, which may again suggest an acceptance of expertise and authority (Table 144).

Discussion groups shed new light on these questions. While it may be true that those who agree to attend a discussion on values and priorities may be somewhat more confident and outspoken than Canadians answering polls, it is clear that participants in groups take far-from-elitist perspectives. They insisted that democracy is failing in large part because they are not adequately informed and included. In this view, democracy means "that the people who are involved all have the same information and that they are given the opportunity to digest and understand the information and to speak about it, to have input." One group noted that the political system worked best when citizens took an active role in debating issues and then let the political elite know how they felt. They agreed that the political system would not change for the better unless people became more active and "forced it" to change.

However, discussion group participants revealed deep paradoxes around the issue of how to get one's voice heard in the current system. There was a consensus in every group that average citizens have very little say in the decisions of government between elections. Similarly, the polling data suggests a strong agreement that the government "must place more emphasis on consulting its citizens" (Table145). At the same time, few believe that consultations have a "real impact on government actions." In discussions, this feeling of helplessness was especially prevalent in the agency-recruited groups.

Where polling data indicates that Canadians may be reluctant to accept that individual citizens bear mutual responsibility for the national crisis (Table 145), discussion group findings

"A lot of people go in there with romantic notions of being able to make changes. Maybe their intentions really are good when they start out and they really think they can make a difference. But then [...] [they] get caught in all the red tape and all the rigamarole. [They] soon lose sight of maybe what [they] went there for because [they're] so busy trying to keep [their] head up."

"The government is looking at or making decisions based on what corporations want and the corporation isn't held responsible. They're given the money but not held responsible."

"The government is not listening to the people, it is listening to outside people, which could be the States [...] or corporations."

"There are times when we have a democracy but I think that in all systems there's going to be times when it fails. We have to look at what our success rate is and decide whether we want to take steps to change it. We are reaching a point where things aren't looking very good and we're going to have to put in some safeguards to have some change."

"I can't believe that if I really, really wanted to do something, that I would have no impact at all. I think I could make my voice heard if I really wanted to. It gets back to what we were talking about, energy and time."

"It still comes back to each one of us who are involved spreading our story, telling people, encouraging those around us to get involved. Because you're a thorn in the Premier's side.

61

suggest that this may reflect a sense of disenfranchisement. Citizens may be reluctant to take the blame when they do not feel authentically involved in the processes by which decisions are taken.

Many Canadians do not know how they can get involved other than voting. One participant said about joining a political party, "I thought you had to be somebody special and pay a lot of money up to the party to get in there."

For many, it takes too much to be involved in bringing about change. Participants in agency-recruited groups noted that being active in a way that brought about change might take more energy, time, knowledge of the system, confidence, and power than many individuals have. They may also be worried about repercussions.

In this context, what from the polls might be interpreted as elitist attitudes or as deference to authority takes on a different cast. In polls, Canadians rank national elections and referenda as the most useful mechanisms of public consultation and express cynicism about royal commissions and public hearings (Table 146). However, discussion group findings suggest that none of the existing mechanisms may adequately engage the public. Participants were frustrated with the mechanisms offered and discouraged about whether or not they would be heard, but they saw themselves as legitimate and important participants in social policy debates.

Many participants across all groups believed that only concerted group effort will bring about change. Many wanted to rebuild community spirit and power. They would value a process of democratization that could offer more information, access to decision makers, increased commitment and control at local levels. At the same time, they recognized that no community can succeed on its own.

Participants saw negative media attention as a lever to make government respond. Some seemed to have more faith in the power of the media than in the democratic process to bring problems and desires to the ears of the politicians.

The process of dialogue created in the discussions offered some participants a new sense of purpose and political leverage. Among participants from family service agencies in particular, several groups ended their discussions with references to new kinds of political actions. These included instances when sole support parents came up with the idea of organizing new political parties focused on their

But if more people can understand the message, the people who vote for him are going to be little thorns in his side too. And it grows and grows and grows. For things to be fair, all of us have to take individual responsibility and educate others."

"If you want government to change something you don't like, call the newspapers [...] You just shine a little light on it and everybody knows what's going on. They are embarrassed, they change it."

"Our group has been a real thorn in his side and they've done everything they can to try and separate and pull us apart because we were an annoyance. But it's a bit like the mosquito that keeps bugging you. It bugs you but when it bites, it's not going to cause you any real great amount of harm. It causes an itch."

concerns. On two occasions, groups pointed out the strengths of particularly articulate and thoughtful participants, encouraging them to run for office. This suggests that the most productive forms of public dialogue may not only encourage people to think more deeply about these issues, but also to engage them in new ways.

"You can say whatever you want. It's not going to make any difference to them. They do what they want."

"If you just go by yourself, they're going to laugh at you."

"If you don't have money, you are not really treated like a human being, especially by government."

Feelings about dialogue and democratization were not uniformly positive. One group in 25 later reported feeling more frustrated after the group dialogue on political participation. In other groups, a small-but-vocal set of participants remained sceptical that citizen input will bring about any change. Some who said they contacted elected representatives, and some others, doubted that information or pressure by citizens brought about real change. In reply to a comment about using the media to embarrass politicians, one participant said, "Oh! they hate it, but how much do they change?"

These findings suggest some deep-seated tensions surrounding issues of democratic engagement. Canadians have generally seen themselves as less disillusioned and bitter about the political process than Americans. The sentiments expressed in these discussion groups suggest that this perceived difference may no longer hold. While Canadians want to be engaged, they feel a growing detachment from those in office and growing powerlessness in the face of political decisions taken without authentic consultation. They have not given up on the political process and on their hopes for fuller involvement, but they voice clear reservations and frustrations about the way things work now.

Epilogue: Next Steps

The restructuring of the social safety net will have profound impacts on Canadian lives. In articulating the values of Canadians as important foundations for well-being, this report is a starting point along several paths. These paths are four-fold. They include: 1) negotiation of principles for social policy reform in the emerging federal-provincial dialogue, 2) encouragement of a continuing public discussion of trade-offs that offers many Canadians the opportunity to reflect on values and principles, 3) development of vehicles to ensure greater accountability to citizens about the realization of values and principles, and 4) sharper research and public education to examine the stereotypes and misinformation that currently hinder more informed public judgment. The following pages examine each of these paths in turn.

Stimulating the Federal-Provincial Dialogue

In the current policy context, the federal government has made a commitment to negotiate principles for guiding the Canadian Health and Social Transfer (CHST) with the provinces. The findings of this report provide a neutral research base for that discussion. CPRN will be available to present the findings of this report to all concerned at conferences, round-tables and other fora, including governments and political interests at all levels, intergovernmental bodies such as the Ministerial Council on Social Policy Reform and Renewal, front-line agencies affected by reforms, professional associations, and others interested in considering Canadian values in the context of social policy reform.

Fostering Public Discussion: The Society We Want

Canadians want a deeper-level democratic engagement in the decisions that affect them. People want to be part of the process of social policy change. As a result, and based on the advice of our Advisory Committee, CPRN is launching a process to encourage broader public dialogue. In the United States, this process has been widely fostered by the Kettering Foundation through its National Issues Forum, which reaches out to approximately 1,000 local groups.

In Canada, the process of public judgment is as yet untested. The findings here indicate that the time is right for launching a public dialogue in Canada. The Canadian public is keenly aware of the key issues in reforming Canadian social policy. Over recent years Canadians have increasingly put the spotlight on social policy issues. They have, over the same period, recognized the need for fiscal reform to reduce government expenditures. The CPRN public dialogue project, modelled on some of the elements of the U.S. process, forms a pilot project in Canada.

The process of fostering public judgment has the potential to help Canadians crystallize core values. This may allow core values to become embedded in both the decision-making process and public discourse. It creates an opportunity for core values and public judgment to become recognized as essential pieces in policymaking and for the technical platform on which decisions are often based to be assessed and balanced by a perspective on Canadian values.

Our current partners in this initiative include the Community Foundations of Canada, the YWCA of Canada, United Way of Canada in direct partnerships with the United Way of Metropolitan Toronto and the United Way of the Lower Midland, Frontier College, the Imagine Campaign of the Centre for Philanthropy, Family Service Canada, the Association of Aboriginal Friendship Circles, the Unitarian Universalist Church of Toronto, and the World Interfaith Association of Ontario.

CPRN will be creating a dialogue kit entitled The Society We Want *that will help all partners and others to organize and carry out discussions. We will also be offering five regional workshops to orient local affiliates of these and other partners All of these partners will engage members of their communities. Exploratory work will be undertaken to amplify these discussions through technological applications, including a WEB site on the Internet, radio phone-in discussions, and televised participation. It is hoped that many more discussions will follow this first wave. The results of further public discussions will be stored at a database site coordinated with a university.*

In addition to this dialogue on a new social contract, CPRN sees the potential for using the processes and tools it has developed for a wide range of other issues, including national unity and local issues related to citizen participation in schools. We will be available to explore these options with interested organizations and sponsors.

Enhancing Accountability

Canadians not only want proof that programs are well-conceived, well-managed, and offer results, but they also want to be informed and engaged in charting future policy and program directions. In order to lay the groundwork for these guarantees, CPRN wants to look at ways to achieve new kinds of accountability in a transformed policy and program environment.

We are developing a discussion paper on the potential elements of a new accountability tool-kit. This paper will include ideas about: 1) how to measure and monitor effectiveness, results, and progress in social policy, and 2) how to best share knowledge and experiences with Canadians across systems and jurisdictions. This project will involve looking at both lessons derived from past experience and the approaches taken in other countries.

Following completion of the paper, CPRN will be holding a policy research symposium, involving academic experts and public officials, in the Spring of 1996. Its objectives will be two-fold: to scope out the mechanisms for accountability faced in the new environment and to assess further research requirements.

Proposing Future Research

Public judgment in Canada is currently in transition. This first report on values raises many issues for future research. These include: 1) the nature of the relationship between the process of public judgement and available information, 2) the extent of difference in how values are articulated into principles by different groups, and 3) time-series data on values and principles. None of these research issues is easily addressed. These ideas are raised for future consideration. CPRN wants to discuss their potential with others in the research and policy community.

To explore the first issue, it will be important to look at the evolution of values in a context that contrasts available stereotypes, misinformation and facts on: a) policy and programs, and b) family demographics and program statistics. For example, the debate on income security, welfare incentive, and single moms would be greatly enhanced by a greater public exposure of the stereotypes and myths revealed by our data relative to the current state of affairs, including information on welfare regimes and the actual demographic.

To explore the second issue, it will be important to examine the relationship between articulated values and demographic factors and to ask more systematically about differences between program recipients and non-recipients. While the polling data here has been examined by demographics where possible, future studies should explore the extent to which group discussion outcomes differ when these groups work together. Similarly, research also needs to be undertaken to discover whether group dynamic effects create important outcome differences, including work with groups of greater heterogeneity to understand the learning process that occurs in groups.

Finally, an area of possible research concerns longitudinal or better time-series data on values and principles. While the polling data cited here covers a wide scope, it does so by raising issues across different surveys at different times. A more coherent values survey across a range of issues conducted over time would be an important addition to knowledge on Canadian values. CPRN will be assessing the viability of more long-term data both in polls and through discussion groups.

Appendices

A *Public Opinion Poll Databases*

The background report on public opinion poll data was compiled by Michael Sullivan and Christine Chalmers of The Strategic Counsel Inc. The following data were consulted:

Angus Reid Group, Inc., *The National Angus Reid Poll* (1993/1994/1995)

Angus Reid Group, Inc., *Social Security Reform Waves I, II and III for HRD Canada* (1994)

Angus Reid Group, Inc., *The State of the Family in Canada* (1994)

Angus Reid Group, Inc., *Canada and the World* (1993)

Angus Reid Group, Inc., *Survey Conducted for Multiculturalism and Citizenship* (1991)

Decima Research, *Survey Conducted for the Canadian Council of Christians and Jews* (1995)

Decima Research, *Decima Quarterly* (1980-1993)

Decima Research, *Survey for Health Canada on Attitudes toward Parenting and Children* (1993)

Decima Research, *Survey Conducted for the Canadian Centre for Philanthropy* (1987)

Ekos Research Associates, Inc., *Rethinking Government ' 94* (1994)

Gallup Canada, *Gallup Poll* (1945-1991)

Goldfarb Consultants, *The Goldfarb Report* (1985)

HayGroup, Opinion Leader Research Program, *Public Sector Issues: Paying the Price* (1995)

Insight Canada, *Perspectives Canada* (1992-1994)

Institute for Social Research, *1993 Canadian National Election Study* (1993)

Institute for Social Research, *1992 National Referendum Study* (1992)

Institute for Social Research, *1988 Canadian National Election Study* (1988)

Institute for Social Research, *Attitudes toward Civil Liberties and the Canadian Charter of Rights* (1987)

Price Waterhouse, *Canada Health Monitor* (1988-1994)

B   Discussion Group Methodology

The discussion groups were coordinated by M-J Wason, an associate of CPRN Inc. Ms. Wason also wrote the background paper to this report on the discussion group findings.

Process

Two hundred and seventy-six group participants were recruited from eight cities across Canada. These were Vancouver, Calgary, Regina, Hamilton, Ottawa, Montreal, Halifax, and Saint John. Participants were recruited in one of two ways: 1) random recruitment with direct digit dialling of Canadians not on social assistance but otherwise distributed by age, sex and employment status, and 2) recruitment by family service agencies or other community serving agencies from among their clientele. This included some discussions held with existing support groups, particularly self-help groups with sole support mothers on social assistance.

Twenty-five groups took place in total. Most were conducted in English, but the two randomly recruited groups held in Montreal were conducted in French. No "agency-recruited" group was held in that city. Only one agency group was held in Ottawa; it was considered a pilot group. Discussions were audiotaped and transcripts were recorded for analysis.

The two- to three-hour in-depth discussions used a range of strategies to give participants opportunities to consider how they would advise on important policy decisions, to reflect on the underlying values that they feel must underpin their choices, and to clarify the most important principles that they feel should inform the decision-making process.

In considering trade-offs, participants were encouraged not just to choose between alternatives, but to explain why they came to that decision. They were assured that the decisions did not have right or wrong answers, and that the group would not necessarily need to come to a consensus. Instead, they were encouraged to develop a dialogue about their underlying values and about the core commitments and principles that they would like to see reflected in decisions about social policies and programs.

In numerous cases, participants commented on the learning process engaged by the discussion – a process by which they sometimes strengthened their resolve to stand by an initial position, sometimes chose an opposing position, or most often refined the parameters of initial positions.

On some issues, related concerns surfaced concerning the availability and accuracy of information necessary to consider the desired value judgments. Some participants called for more information. When new details were offered in the group by other participants, it was often incorporated into the discussion. If requested, facilitators clarified or established a more accurate or up-to-date basis for discussion, but they did not routinely intervene. As a result, the so-called "facts" offered to groups by participants sometimes involved misinformation, stereotypes, and myths related to public policy issues. This sometimes led to debates among participants. Often, however, this information, especially when presented in an authoritative manner, was likely to be accepted at face value by group members. Many participants expressed frustration that the public information available to make decisions seemed to them incomplete, outdated, or inaccurate. In order to realize their values, they wanted clearer situational information on the context of the choices before them. This also sparked recognitions of the need for more public information.

Most participants stressed the importance of engaging in a process by which they could be helped to think about their values. At the end of almost all discussion groups, participants expressed their appreciation at having a forum where they could voice their opinions, clarify opinions and resolve judgments. They saw this as a different kind of exercise than any in which they had previously engaged. All but a few requested follow-up information on the project, and volunteered to be further involved in activities related to this or other projects dealing with the values of Canadians. In groups recruited from family service agencies especially, the predominant feeling after group discussion was a greater sense of power and involvement. A number of these groups discussed their desire to become more involved and politically active on their own. In one family service agency group, however, the group process may have had a backlash impact. While positive at the time, those participants later expressed fear, insecurity, and increased frustration at confronting these issues to their regular group leader.

Participant Characteristics

Two hundred and seventy-six participants filled out a descriptive questionnaire just prior to the discussion group. A few late arrivals did not fill out questionnaires. Of these, 125 (47%) were recruited through the Family Service Canada agency network and 142 (53%) were recruited through a process of random digit dialling. Full demographics are provided in the background paper by M-J Wason.

The majority (78%) of participants were between the ages of 21 and 50. Most agency-recruited participants were 31- 40 years old, compared to 41-50 in randomly-recruited groups. Over 89% of participants in agency groups were female, reflecting recruitment of sole support mothers on social assistance, while both genders were equally represented in random groups; 61% of the randomly recruited participants were married. Participants in the agency-recruited groups had a mean average of 1.48 other family members living in their household. Participants in the "randomly-recruited" groups had a slightly higher mean average of 1.94. Almost two-thirds of all respondents had received some post-secondary or trade training. Significantly, more participants in the "agency-recruited" groups had not completed high school. Significantly, more participants in the "randomly-recruited" groups were university graduates.

Respondents were asked to estimate their total combined 1994 annual income, from all sources before deductions, of all family members. The majority of agency-recruited participants (84%) had incomes of less than $29,999 per year whereas the majority of "randomly-recruited" participants (78%) reported incomes between $20,000 and $79,999.

There were significantly more members (71%) of the agency-recruited groups who had annual incomes of less than $19,999. Only 11% of randomly-recruited participants had family incomes at this level. Of the randomly recruited, 72% earned over $30,000 per year, and only 16% of agency participants.

Participants in the randomly-recruited groups were more likely to receive their income from salary, income from self-employment, pensions, and investments than participants in the agency-recruited groups. Those members of the agency-recruited groups were more likely to receive their income from social assistance and child support or alimony than members of the other group. Two-thirds of the members of the agency-recruited groups noted that social assistance was one of the sources of their family's income.

Half of all participants were not working for pay. Randomly-recruited group members were more likely to be working and working full-time. Agency-recruited group members were more likely not to be working for pay and if working, working part-time. In Hamilton, significantly more people were not working for pay than the average.

Significantly more members of the randomly-recruited groups spent much of their waking hours working for pay. Significantly more members of agency-recruited groups spend their waking hours in care of their own children.

The vast majority of participants (91%) were born in Canada. Between 10 and 13% of all respondents identified themselves as a member of a First Nation, visible minority or racial group. The most common language generally spoken in participants' home was English. In Montreal, 13 of the 15 participants spoke French at home. Cree, Mohawk, Tagalog, Gujarati, sign language, Spanish, Dutch, and Chinese were also reported as languages used at home. There were significantly more agency-recruited participants who identified themselves as a person with a disability other than a physical disability.

Assisting Community Service Agencies and Groups

Don Karst
Calgary Family Service Bureau, Calgary, Alberta

Greg Campbell
Mike McKernan
Catholic Family Service, Calgary, Alberta

Monica Chaperlin
Community Health Centre, Saint John, New Brunswick

Frank Gibson
Dartmouth Work Activities Society, Dartmouth, Nova Scotia

Eileen McLaughlin
Family Resource Centre, Saint John, New Brunswick

Joyce Halpern
Family Service Association, Halifax, Nova Scotia

Corinne Bokitch
Family Service Bureau of Regina, Regina, Saskatchewan

Maggie Fietz
Family Service Canada, Ottawa, Ontario

Barbara Brett
Ian Mass
Family Services of Greater Vancouver, Vancouver, British Columbia

John Vedell
Ingrid Spence
Family Services of Hamilton-Wentworth, Inc., Hamilton, Ontario

David Buchanan
Heather Maughan
Family Services Saint John, Inc., Saint John, New Brunswick

Mike Meyers
Karen Bridger-Acker
Hamilton Catholic Family Services, Hamilton, Ontario

Elaine Rabin
Kerry Nolan
Jewish Family Services, Ottawa, Ontario

Pam Coates
One Voice for All, Saint John, New Brunswick

Sister Joan O'Keefe
Single Parent Centre, Halifax, Nova Scotia

C   Funders and Advisors

CPRN Core Funders

Canadian International Development Agency
Citizenship and Immigration
Fisheries and Oceans
Health Canada
Human Resources Development Canada
Transport Canada

Project Funders

Ministry of Social Services, British Columbia
Ministry of Community and Social Services, Ontario
Health Canada
Human Resources Development Canada
The National Forum on Health
The Walter and Duncan Gordon Charitable Foundation
The Kahanoff Foundation
The Laidlaw Foundation
The J.W. McConnell Family Foundation

Advisory Group Members

Tom Atkinson, Toronto
David Cameron, University of Toronto
Alfred Carr, Government of Ontario
John Dossetor, The National Forum on Health
Frank Fedyk, Health Canada
Maggie Fietz, Family Service Canada
Nathan Gilbert, Laidlaw Foundation
Arlene Hoffman, Government of Ontario
Judith Maxwell, CPRN Inc.
Ian McKinnon, Pacific Enterprises Ltd.

Jan Mears, Government of B.C.
George Perlin, Queen's University
Gordon Roberts, Human Resources Development Canada
Lyn Tait, Government of B.C.
Marian Walsh, Metro Toronto Home Care
Cynthia Williams, Human Resources Development Canada

Project Team

Suzanne Peters, The Policy Research Group and CPRN Inc.
Marian Botsford Fraser, E•Y•E Inc.
Christine Chalmers, The Strategic Counsel, Inc.
Michael Sullivan, The Strategic Counsel, Inc.
M-J Wason, CPRN Inc.
Eric Young, E•Y•E Inc.

Additional Commentators

Margaret Biggs, CPRN Inc.
Michael Hall, The Canadian Centre for Philanthropy

Tables

Table 1 — Model of Society

	March-August 1987	
	General Public %	Elites %
A unified body pursuing a common goal	49	37
Neither	15	32
A collection of people independently pursuing their own goals	29	27

➤ Older Canadians and those with less education, as well as those born outside of Canada, are more likely to say that Canadian society should act as a unified body.

Q. Ideally, Canadian society should be like:
Source: Institute for Social Research, Attitudes toward Civil Liberties and the Canadian Charter of Rights.

Table 2 — Reliance on Government

	February 1989	
	Agree %	Disagree %
People are responsible for their own lives. Every person must save by himself for his own old age, disability or retirement.	64	36
The government has a responsibility to insure that all citizens have the basic necessities of life, regardless of circumstances.	84	15

➤ Those who have received welfare or social assistance, and those living in the Atlantic and Prairie provinces, are least likely to agree that "people are responsible for their own lives." Quebecers are most likely to agree.

➤ No significant demographic differences on "government has a responsibility."

Q. Do you agree, strongly agree, disagree or strongly disagree with the following statement?
Source: Gallup Canada, The Gallup Poll.

Table 3 — Public Policy Priorities (1988-1995)

	Nov. 1988 %	Nov. 1989 %	Nov. 1990 %	Nov. 1991 %	Nov. 1992 %	Nov. 1993 %	Dec. 1994 %	Feb. 1995 %	Mar. 1995 %	May 1995 %	June 1995 %	July 1995 %
Unemployment/ jobs	11	8	9	27	37	58	28	29	28	31	35	34
Deficit/debt	5	10	10	10	12	33	20	48	35	25	28	28
National unity/ Quebec	-	-	13	26	6	4	33	35	25	21	24	22
The economy (general)	6	9	29	42	63	21	21	20	21	20	18	22
Health care/ social services*	9	5	3	4	7	14	10	13	18	20	19	19
Health care	n/a	n/a	n/a	n/a	n/a	9	5	7	11	14	12	12
Poverty	2	5	3	5	5	3	7	5	6	7	8	8
Taxes	6	31	35	11	3	5	6	13	6	7	5	5
Social services	n/a	n/a	n/a	n/a	n/a	5	5	6	7	6	7	7
Crime/justice	1	3	1	2	2	2	8	7	6	6	9	11
Gun control	-	-	-	-	-	-	1	2	1	6	3	1
Education	9	3	1	2	6	5	5	6	7	6	5	3
Immigration	1	2	2	2	2	3	4	4	3	4	4	3
Environment	10	24	14	8	7	5	2	3	4	3	5	4
International issues	0	3	13	1	1	1	1	0	1	3	4	1
Defence/peace	2	2	1	1	1	1	1	1	1	2	1	2
Government/ politics	2	4	7	4	5	3	1	2	3	2	2	3
Free trade/trade	70	9	4	5	4	16	1	2	2	2	2	1
Fishing	-	-	-	-	-	-	-	-	7	1	1	2
Other economic issues	2	3	2	1	3	1	1	1	1	1	2	1
Native issues	2	2	8	3	3	1	2	1	1	1	2	3
Moral issues	-	-	-	1	1	1	1	0	1	1	1	1
Abortion	9	16	2	1	0	0	1	0	0	0	0	1
Constitution	1	23	9	22	8	2	0	0	0	0	0	0
Language issues	1	4	5	3	2	1	0	0	0	0	0	0
Racism	-	-	-	1	1	1	0	0	0	0	0	0
Other	17	17	6	4	5	6	6	5	13	7	7	5

Q.   *Thinking of the issues presently confronting Canada, I'd like to know which one you feel requires the greatest attention from the country's leaders.*
Note: * *These two items were presented together in previous soundings. Above, mentions for each are reported separately for Nov. 1993 onwards. "Other" includes policy issues mentioned by less than 1% of all respondents. Up to 3 mentions were accepted.*
Source: *Angus Reid Group, Inc., The National Angus Reid Poll, "National Standards for Social Programs."*

Table 4 — *Evaluation of Program Cuts: Medicare*

	July/August 1993 %	Good thing %	Bad thing %
Medicare:			
Will be essentially the same as it is today	12	94	4
Will still be in place but will provide more limited coverage	65	40	56
Will no longer exist	21	12	86

Q. Let's think for a moment about Canada's universal health care program - medicare. Looking ahead to when you yourself are elderly, what do you think the medicare program will be like by that time? Do you think when you are elderly...
Source: Angus Reid Group, Inc., The National Angus Reid Poll.

Table 5 — *Spending on Social Programs*

	June 1994 Agree %	Disagree %
I'm personally very concerned about the future of our social safety net programs.	78	10
When I hear the federal government is going to reform our social programs, I'm worried that people who really need them would be hurt.	73	17
I'm concerned that more and more people are falling through the cracks and are not being helped by today's social programs.	59	22

Q. On a scale from "1" to "7," where "1" means you strongly disagree and "7" means you strongly agree, to what extent do you agree or disagree with the following statements?   Agree = 5,6,7/Disagree = 1,2,3
Source: Angus Reid Group, Social Security Reform Wave II for Human Resources Development Canada.

Table 6 — Willingness to Accept Cuts in Services

	Spring 1990 %	Spring 1991 %
Freezing Provincial Education and Health Payments:		
Very upset	44	44
Somewhat upset	36	33
Not very upset	10	13
Not upset at all	10	10

➤ Atlantic Canadians (55%) and British Columbians (50%) more likely to be very upset. Ontarians (41%) and Quebecers (39%) least likely to be very upset.

➤ Women (48%), and middle-aged Canadians (47%) more likely to express concern.

Q.   There are a number of specific things that the federal government did in the budget in order to reduce the deficit or promote economic growth in Canada. I'm going to name some of these things and I'd like you to tell me if you are very upset, somewhat upset, not very upset or not upset at all that the government has done these things? How about frozen the amount of money that it gives to the province for things like health care and education?
Source: Decima Research, Decima Quarterly.

Table 7 — Deficit Reduction and Program Cuts

	1993 %
We must reduce the deficit even if that means cutting programmes.	54
Governments must maintain programmes even if that means continuing to run a deficit.	34

➤ University-educated more likely to say we must reduce deficit. Older Canadians also more deficit-focused, as are men.

Q.   On the deficit, which comes closest to your own view?
Source: Carleton University/Institute for Social Research, Canadian National Election Study.

Table 8 — Attitudes toward Specific Spending Cuts — Fall 1992

	Increase taxes %	Increase deficit %	Cut spending %
Hospital services	31	33	32
Primary and secondary education	30	35	32
Income support for senior citizens	29	38	30
Programs for disabled	29	42	24
Income support for unemployable	26	35	34
Post-secondary education	23	34	39
Children's benefits	23	33	39
Doctors' services	15	20	60
Income support for unemployed	14	28	54

Q   *How about …? Which one of the following three options would you personally choose if this program or service was in financial trouble? Would you increase taxes, increase government spending and the deficit, or cut spending?*
Source: Decima Research, Decima Quarterly.

Table 9 — View on Social Program Reform

	1994 %
With unemployment the way it is these days, now is not the time to make changes to our social programs.	25
Now is as good a time as any to make changes to our social programs.	72

➤   Those living in the Atlantic region and those with some high-school education are more likely to feel first statement is closest to their point of view. Those who have graduated from university or college were less likely.

➤   Those with some high-school education less likely to feel second statement is closest to their point of view.

Q.   *Which of the following statements is closest to your own point of view?*
Source: Angus Reid Group, Inc., Research conducted on behalf of Human Resources Development Canada, 1994.

Table 10 — Attitudes Toward Social Program Reform

	1994	
	% agreeing (5,6, 7)	% disagreeing (1,2,3)
Young employable people should no longer be eligible to receive unemployment insurance or welfare. Instead, they should receive education, training and a small living allowance.	79	12
When I hear the federal government is going to reform our social programs, I'm worried that people who really need them would be hurt.	71	32
The existence of our social programs makes it too easy for people to give up looking for work.	69	20
Knowing that the social programs are available gives me a real sense of security.	59	25
If people just took more responsibility for themselves and their families, we wouldn't need all of these social programs.	57	30
I'm concerned that more and more people are falling through the cracks and are not being helped by today's social programs.	56	27
I'd be prepared to reduce the quality and accessibility of our social programs if it means we could reduce taxes.	53	31
There is not much point in making major reforms to Canada's social programs until there are more jobs for people who want to work.	42	44
With so many people living in poverty today, we should be talking about providing more rather than less generous program benefits.	43	42

Q: On a scale from 1 to 7, where "1" means you strongly disagree and "7" means you strongly agree, to what extent do you agree or disagree with the following statements?
Source: Angus Reid Group, Research conducted on behalf of Human Resources Development Canada, 1994.

Table 10 (Cont'd.) — *Attitudes Toward Social Program Reform among Population Groupings*

When I hear the federal government is going to reform our social programs, I'm worried that people who really need them would be hurt.

More likely to agree
> Residents of Quebec, those with some high-school education

Knowing that the social programs are available gives me a real sense of security.

Less likely to agree
> Residents of Alberta

More likely to agree
> Residents of Quebec, those age 55 plus years, those with some high-school education

If people just took more responsibility for themselves and their families, we wouldn't need all of these social programs.

Less likely to agree
> Those under the age of 25 years

More likely to agree
> Residents of Quebec

I'd be prepared to reduce the quality and accessibility of our social programs if it means we could reduce taxes.

Less likely to agree
> Residents of Alberta

There is not much point in making major reforms to Canada's social programs until there are more jobs for people who want to work.

Less likely to agree
> Residents of British Columbia and Alberta, those who have graduated university or college

With so many people living in poverty today, we should be talking about providing more rather than less generous program benefits.

Less likely to agree
> Those who have graduated from university or college

More likely to agree
> Residents of the Atlantic region, those under 25 years of age

Table 11 — Descriptions of Social Programs

1994

	% agreeing Wave I	% agreeing Wave II	% disagreeing Wave I	% disagreeing Wave II
In need of reform	84	-	5	-
Too easy for people to abuse	81	-	10	-
Essential	78	74	8	14
Helps people in time of need	79	69	9	17
In crisis	69	-	14	-
An important part of our Canadian identity	70	-	14	-
Helps people who really need it	67	-	20	-
Too expensive given the size of our deficit	59	57	23	27
Makes people dependent	66	-	18	-
Not designed to meet the current and future needs of our economy	62	57	16	22
Wasteful	53	-	30	-
Easy to access for legitimate applicants	64	-	17	-
Not designed to meet the current and future needs of Canadian families	56	-	20	-
A luxury we can no longer afford	40	-	43	-
Compassionate	44	50	32	28
Part of our past, but not part of our future	38	36	39	42
Provides assistance to prepare people for employment	41	-	38	-
Effective	44	30	32	46
Efficient	20	29	57	60

Q.   I am now going to read to you some words and phrases that people have used to describe Canada's social programs. I would like you to tell me whether you agree or disagree that the phrase describes Canada's social programs on a scale from 1 to 7 where "1" means you strongly disagree and "7" means you strongly agree that the phrase describes Canada's social programs. A "4" means you do not agree or disagree. The first one is…
Source: Angus Reid Group, Social Security Reform Waves I and II for Human Resource Development Canada. (Agree=5,6,7/ Disagree=1,2,3)

Table 12 — Reasons for Poverty

	March-August 1987	
	General public %	Elites %
They don't try hard enough to get ahead	16	11
Neither	51	72
The wealthy and powerful keep them poor	24	13

➤ Those with less education and lower incomes are more likely to say the poor are kept poor.

Q. The poor are poor because:
Source: Institute for Social Research, Attitudes toward Civil Liberties and the Canadian Charter of Rights.

Table 13 — Perceived Effectiveness in Eradicating Poverty

	Fall 1990 %
Totally agree	49
Agree somewhat	31
Neutral	10
Disagree somewhat	6
Disagree totally	4
Mean (-5 to +5)	3.09

➤ Quebecers most in agreement, British Columbians least in agreement.

➤ University-educated, youngest Canadians least in agreement.

Q. I'd like you to tell me how you personally feel about this statement by giving me a number between minus 5 and plus 5, where -5 means you totally disagree with the statement and +5 means you totally agree with the statement. Many people's opinions fall somewhere in between these two points depending on how they feel about the statement. The statement is: No matter what society and governments do, there will always be poor people in Canada.
Source: Decima Research, Decima Quarterly.

Table 14 — Perceived Effectiveness of Child Policy

November 1993

	Programs to help children in low-income families will end up making people more dependent on government.		Government programs and policies can do little to solve the problems that children face.	
	General public %	Parents %	General public %	Parents %
Strongly agree	12 } 38	11 } 36	6 } 27	5 } 25
Agree	26	25	21	20
Neutral	38	39	40	40
Disagree	17	18	23	24
Strongly disagree	6	17	10	11

Q. *I'm now going to read you a number of statements about issues related to children and parents. For each one, I'd like you to tell me whether you agree or disagree with it using a 0-10 scale, where "0" means you strongly disagree and "10" means you strongly agree with the statement. The first one is...*

Source: *Decima Research, A Decima Research Report to Health Canada on Attitudes Toward Parenting and Children.*

Table 15 — Reliance on Government

March-August 1987

	General public %	Elites %
Strongly agree	11	6
Agree	47	45
Disagree	22	30
Strongly disagree	10	11

➤ Those with lower household incomes and seniors are most likely to agree they are glad they have a government that looks after them.

Q. *I am glad that I have a government that looks after me in so many ways.*

Source: *Institute for Social Research, Attitudes toward Civil Liberties and the Canadian Charter of Rights.*

Table 16 — Reliance on Government

	February 1989	
	Agree %	Disagree %
People are responsible for their own lives. Every person must save by himself for his own old age, disability or retirement.	64	36
The government has a responsibility to insure that all citizens have the basic necessities of life, regardless of circumstances.	84	15

➤ Those who have received welfare or social assistance, and those living in the Atlantic and Prairie provinces, are least likely to agree that "people are responsible for their own lives." Quebecers are most likely to agree.

➤ No significant demographic differences on "government has a responsibility."

Q. *Do you agree, strongly agree, disagree or strongly disagree with the following statement?*
Source: Gallup Canada, The Gallup Poll.

Table 17 — Reduction of Income Gap

	1993 %
Strongly agree	28
Agree	39
Disagree	24
Strongly disagree	6

➤ Atlantic Canadians, Quebecers, those with less education, and women are more likely to agree.

➤ Ontarians, the university educated, and men less likely to agree.

Q. *The government must do more to reduce the income gap between rich and poor Canadians.*
Source: Carleton University/Institute for Social Research, Canadian National Election Studies.

Table 18 — Responsibility for the Poor and Aging

September 1993

	Government has a responsibility for the poor %	Government has a responsibility for the elderly %
Germany	97	95
Russia	95	96
Italy	95	96
Taiwan	93	92
Spain	92	90
United Kingdom	91	93
Singapore	90	86
Hong Kong	90	94
Japan	85	88
Canada	83	86
Australia	82	85
Korea	82	76
France	79	69
India	72	55
United States	69	75
Mexico	46	68

Source: Angus Reid Group, Canada and the World.

Table 19 — Role of Government

	February 1994	
	General public Mean (0 to 100)	**Elites Mean** (0 to 100)
To protect Canadians from crime and abuse.	86.5	77.0
To do whatever is necessary to ensure full employment for whoever is willing and able to work.	84.9	61.5
To work with Canadians to build a country which can be a source of pride to all citizens and a model for the world	84.4	68.1
To plan for the future generations.	82.9	72.0
To work more closely in partnership with business, labour and individual citizens to come up with shared solutions.	82.0	69.6
To do whatever is necessary to ensure the highest possible financial standard of living for the citizens of Canada.	80.1	64.0
To promote the highest possible overall quality of life for the citizens of Canada, including both financial and idealistic concerns.	79.4	65.8
To promote tolerance and understanding throughout Canadian society.	77.2	61.9
To promote a fair and efficient marketplace for business and consumers.	77.1	73.8
To act as a sort of referee ensuring everybody plays by the same rules.	71.8	68.1
To provide the bare minimal presence in order to allow people to get on with their own affairs.	69.2	71.5
To act as a guardian of the public interest in business affairs.	67.6	56.7
To redistribute wealth in order to maintain social equality.	67.3	42.8
To demonstrate Canadian values to people of other countries by having programs for peace-keeping, promotion of democracy and human rights, and the provision of help to the poor in the Third World.	66.7	50.9

Q. Some of the traditional roles of government are under pressure and some people are expecting different things from government in the future. I am going to read you a list of possible future roles for government. For each one, I would like you to rate how appropriate you think that role will be on a scale from 0 to 100 where 0 is not at all appropriate, the midpoint 50 means somewhat appropriate and 100 means extremely appropriate.
Source: Ekos Research Associates, Rethinking Government '94.

Table 20 — View on National Standards by Region

July/August 1995

	Canadians have a right to expect a minimum level of service wherever they live/Need national standards %	Provinces are best able to decide what services are needed/Do *not* need national standards %
Canada	60	36
British Columbia	61	33
Alberta	66	32
Manitoba/Saskatchewan	59	35
Ontario	65	31
Quebec	48	49
Atlantic	68	30

Q. *(Exact wording not available.) Which view is closer to your own?*
Source: *Angus Reid Group*, The Angus Reid Report, *July 1, 1995.*

Table 21 — National Standards for Specific Social Programs

July/August 1995

	Health care like welfare %	University and college education %	Social assistance %
Very essential	80	56	36
Somewhat essential	14	32	42
Not very essential	3	7	14
Not at all essential	2	4	6

➤ With respect to health care and education, Quebecers are less likely to see national standards as very essential. Atlantic Canadians are most likely to see it as very essential. On social assistance, western Canadians are least likely to see this as very essential; Atlantic Canadians most likely.

Q. *As you may have heard, the recent federal budget announced some changes in the way that government programs will be funded. Federal funding to the provinces for university and college education, health care, and social services like welfare, will now be sent as one "lump sum" payment to each province so they can provide services to their residents. The federal government has said it will work with the provinces to develop national principles and objectives for these services. I'd like to ask you some questions about specific services. For each one, I'd like you to tell me how essential it is, in your view that there be national standards of services for all Canadians, regardless of where they live.*
Source *Angus Reid Group, Inc.*, The National Angus Reid Poll, *"National Standards for Social Programs."*

Table 22 — View on National Standards by Region

	July/August 1995 % agreeing
Canada	54
British Columbia	50
Alberta	52
Manitoba/Saskatchewan	46
Ontario	58
Quebec	50
Atlantic	70

Q.   *If the provinces and federal government can't agree on national standards of service to be provided to all Canadians, the federal government should establish the standards itself, and withhold money from the provinces who don't meet those standards.*
Source: Angus Reid Group, The Angus Reid Report, July/August, 1995.

Table 23 — Views on Jurisdiction

	June 1994	
	Should provide job training and counselling services	Should provide social assistance and social services
	%	%
Federal government	26	35
Provincial government	51	42
Both	20	20

Q.   *Which level of government…*
Source: Angus Reid Group, Social Security Reform Wave II for Human Resources Development Canada.

Table 24 — Views on Jurisdiction

	Composite Scores	
	1991 %	**1992** %
Federal	35	44
Provincial	51	38
Both	8	15

Q.   *Preferred level of government for setting and enforcing health standards and delivering health services.*
Source: Price Waterhouse, The Canada Health Monitor.

Table 25 — Trust in Reform Process

	June 1994 %
Strongly agree	11
Agree	23
Neutral	19
Disagree	25
Strongly disagree	22

➤ Albertans were less likely to agree with this statement, while those with annual incomes of less than $20K were more likely to agree.

Q.   *I trust the federal government to make the changes that are necessary to reform our social programs.*
Source: Angus Reid Group, Social Security Reform Wave II for Human Resources Development.

Table 26 — Views on Government Motivations Behind Social Program Reform

	1994 %
... it genuinely wants to improve their efficiency and effectiveness	27
... it wants to cut costs by reducing benefits	61
Both	9

➤ Young Canadians (<25 years) more likely to state that "it wants to cut costs by reducing benefits" is closer to their point of view.

Q.   Some people say the main reasons that the federal government is reforming our social programs is because…Which statement is closest to your point of view?
Source: Angus Reid Group, Research conducted on behalf of Human Resources Development, 1994.

Table 27 — Collective Responsibility

| | November 1993 | | | |
| | General population | | Parents | |
	Agree %	Disagree %	Agree %	Disagree %
It is the parents' responsibility, not anyone else's, to look after the health and well-being of children.	66	12	67	12
I think we have to rely less on governments for solving society's problems.	61	14	58	16
I don't feel I have any personal responsibility to be involved in the lives of children who are not my own.	16	55	13	62

➤ Men more likely than women to agree we should rely less on government to solve our problems.
➤ Older Canadians more likely than younger Canadians to take an individualist stance with respect to children and parenting.
➤ Those with less education are more likely to take an individualist stance.

Q.   *I'm now going to read you a number of statements about issues related to children and parents. For each one, I'd like you to tell me whether you agree or disagree with it using a 0-10 scale, where "0" means you strongly disagree and "10" means you strongly agree with the statement. The first one is...*
Source: *Decima Research, A Decima Research Report to Health Canada on Attitudes toward Parenting and Children.*

Table 28 — Values Placed on Parenting and Children

| | November 1993 | | | |
| | General population | | Parents | |
	Agree %	Disagree %	Agree %	Disagree %
Children are important to society in their own right, not just because they will grow up to become productive adults.	84	n/a	88	n/a
Being a parent is the most demanding role there is.	82	n/a	84	n/a
Society doesn't place enough value on the contribution made by good parents.	63	n/a	64	n/a
Parents today are not as prepared to make sacrifices for their children as parents of 20 or 25 years ago.	43	29	38	34
All things considered, parents today are doing a very good job raising their children.	35	13	38	12
I don't think parents receive enough help or support in raising their children.	33	25	36	24
Parenting comes naturally, so parents don't really need advice from experts or others on how to raise children.	16	57	12	62

Q.   *I'm now going to read you a number of statements about issues related to children and parents. For each one, I'd like you to tell me whether you agree or disagree with it using a 0-10 scale, where "0" means you strongly disagree and "10" means you strongly agree with the statement. The first one is…*

Source: *Decima Research, A Decima Research Report to Health Canada on Attitudes toward Parenting and Children.*

Table 29 — Willingness to Give to Others' Children

	November 1993			
	General population		Parents	
	Agree %	Disagree %	Agree %	Disagree %
It is the parents' responsibility, not anyone else's, to look after the health and well-being of children.	66	12	67	12
I would be willing to pay more for programs and services to help parents raise their children.	30	38	30	39
I don't feel I have any personal responsibility to be involved in the lives of children who are not my own.	16	55	13	62

➤ Those with higher household incomes are more likely to feel a sense of responsibility for others' children. Still, less than 1 in 20 among those of higher income agree strongly that they would be willing to pay more in taxes for government programs and services aimed at children.

➤ Quebecers particularly unlikely to say they are willing to pay more.

Q. I'm now going to read you a number of statements about issues related to children and parents. For each one, I'd like you to tell me whether you agree or disagree with it using a 0-10 scale, where "0" means you strongly disagree and "10" means you strongly agree with the statement. The first one is...
Source: Decima Research, A Decima Research Report to Health Canada on Attitudes toward Parenting and Children.

Table 30 — *Financial Assistance for Care of Children/Elderly at Home*

	June 1994	
	Agree	Disagree
	%	%
If I heard the government was going to provide financial assistance to help one parent in a two-parent family stay at home to raise their children, I'd think this was good news.	57	29
The government should provide financial assistance to allow people to stay at home to look after elderly family members.	48	33

Q.   On a scale from "1" to "7," where "1" means you strongly disagree and "7" means you strongly agree, to what extent do you agree or disagree with the following statements? (Agree: 5,6,7/Disagree: 1,2,3)
Source: Angus Reid Group, Social Security Reform Wave II for Human Resources Development Canada.

Table 31 — *Reduction of Social Programs Through Self-Reliance*

	June 1994
	%
Strongly agree	27
Agree	28
Neutral	13
Disagree	17
Strongly disagree	14

➤ Respondents age 50 and above are more likely to agree strongly with this statement.

Q.   If people just took more responsibility for themselves and their families we wouldn't need all of these social programs.
Source: Angus Reid Group, Social Security Reform Wave II for Human Resources Development Canada.

Table 32 — Need for Less Dependence on Government

	July 1994 %
Agree	76
Neither agree nor disagree	13
Disagree	10
Mean (1 to 7)	5.48

➤ Younger Canadians (16-24 years) are less likely to agree. Canadians aged 45-54 years and those with annual incomes of $70K or more are more likely to agree.

Q. *More and more people are going to have to stop depending on our federal government and learn to fend for themselves.*
Source: *Ekos Research Associates, Rethinking Government '94.*

Table 33 — Views on Cheating

	June 1994 % agreeing
The existence of our social programs makes it too easy for people to give up looking for work.	68
I think the stories about people cheating our social programs are exaggerated – most people follow the rules.	36

➤ Quebecers and those earning less than $20K annually, were less likely to feel that social programs make it easier for people to give up looking for work.

Q. *On a scale from "1" to "7", where "1" means you strongly disagree and "7" means you strongly agree, to what extent do you agree or disagree with the following statements?*
Source: *Angus Reid Group, Social Security Reform Wave II for Human Resources Development Canada.*

Table 34 — Perceived Effectiveness of Welfare Policies

	Fall 1984 %
Totally agree	29
Agree somewhat	35
Neutral	19
Disagree somewhat	10
Disagree totally	5
Mean (scale -5 to +5)	2.11

➤ Prairies and British Columbia, men, those with university education, those in higher income quintiles, and middle-aged Canadians are most likely to agree.

➤ Quebec, women, those with less education, those in lower income quintiles, and seniors are least likely to agree.

Q.   Welfare kills initiative (exact wording of question not available).
Source: Decima Research, Decima Quarterly.

Table 35 — Views on Disincentives of Unemployment Insurance

	February 1989 %
Agree	56
Disagree	40

Q.   Do you agree or disagree with those people who state that the present system of unemployment insurance encourages people not to work?
Source: Gallup Canada, The Gallup Poll.

Table 36 — Views on Efficiency of Welfare System

	Fall 1992 %
Major decrease	20
Minor decrease	28
No real change	22
Minor increase	16
Major increase	13

➤ Ontario residents were more likely to state that these measures would lead to "major" decreases in the number of people who receive social assistance for long periods of time. Residents of the Atlantic region and British Columbia were more likely to indicate that it would lead to a "minor" decrease.

Q. Many people believe that money by itself will not solve the problems of poverty and social inequality, and that governments would be far better off to give the poor access to education, training, day care and other opportunities that would allow them to stand on their own two feet. If governments did this, do you think that this would lead to a major increase, a minor increase, no real change, a minor decrease or a major decrease in the number of people who receive social assistance for long periods of time?
Source: Decima Research, Decima Quarterly.

Table 37 — Views on Efficiency of Welfare System

	Fall 1990 %	Spring 1992 %
Provide poor with more income	12	9
Provide poor with access to programs	86	90

➤ Quebecers disproportionately likely to say "provide more income" (24%).

➤ Those with less education, and those in the lowest income quintile are more likely to say "provide more income."

Q. Some people say that problems of poverty and social inequality are mainly a question of money - that is, if government simply provided the poor with more income, the problem would be virtually solved. Others say that money by itself will not solve the problems of poverty and social inequality and governments would be far better off to give the poor access to education, day care and the opportunities that would allow them to stand on their own two feet. Which one of these two views best represents your own?
Source: Decima Research, Decima Quarterly.

Table 38 — Views on Guaranteed Annual Income

	% saying "favour" a guaranteed annual income
Summer 1980	66
Spring 1981	74
Fall 1982	67
Fall 1984	73
Fall 1985	77
Fall 1990	67
Winter 1991	68
Historical average:	70

➤ More likely to favour in Quebec (78%); least likely in Ontario (66%).

➤ Women more favourable (74%) than men (67%).

➤ Those with less education more likely to favour. Those in the lowest income quintile more likely to favour (81%); those in the top income quintile are least likely to favour (59%).

➤ Older and younger Canadians more likely to favour than the middle-aged.

Q. (Exact question wording not available.)
Source: Decima Research, Decima Quarterly.

Table 39 — Guaranteed Annual Income for those Receiving Social Assistance

	November 1994 %
Strongly agree	13
Somewhat agree	20
Somewhat disagree	23
Strongly disagree	42

➤ Albertans are less likely to agree and Quebec more likely to agree than the norm. Higher income households are no less likely to agree with this proposition.

Q.   The government has said that one of its goals in reforming social programs is to help people get off welfare by making it easier for them to hold a job. In addition, they want to help the working poor, such as those who have minimum wage jobs, to keep them working and prevent them from going on welfare. I'm going to read you a number of different options for doing this. For each one, I'd like you to tell me if you strongly agree, somewhat agree, somewhat disagree, or strongly disagree with the government implementing this option.... Providing a Guaranteed Annual Income, that is all individuals and families would be guaranteed a basic minimum income whether or not they worked.
Source: Angus Reid Group, Social Security Reform Wave III for Human Resources Development Canada.

Table 40 — *Expectations for Unemployed*

	September 1962 %	June 1976 %
Agree: Should be required to take work	79	86
Disagree: Should be required to take work	14	9

➤ In 1976, no demographic differences.

➤ In 1962, less educated were more likely to agree with the exception of university *graduates*, who were also more likely to agree. In 1962, Quebecers were least likely to agree.

Q.   *Some people believe that an employable man who is receiving relief assistance should be required to undertake any available work. Others disagree. What is your opinion?*
Source: Gallup Canada, The Gallup Poll.

Table 41 — *Expectations for Unemployed*

	1993 %
People on welfare who are physically able should be required to work.	89
Undecided.	7
Requiring people on welfare to work will end up taking jobs away from other people.	3

➤ Those from the Atlantic region were more likely to feel the first statement was closest to their own point of view.

➤ Those earning less than $20K annually were less likely to feel the first statement was closest to their point of view.

➤ No demographic variances for second statement.

Q.   *Which comes closest to your own view?*
Source: Carleton University/Institute for Social Research, Canadian National Election Studies.

Table 42 — Benefits to All or Needy Only

	Government benefits should go only to needy %	Government benefits should go to everyone %
Spring 1981	64	35
Fall 1982	56	42
Spring 1983	59	39
Fall 1984	62	38
Fall 1985	61	38
Fall 1986	61	38
Fall 1990	54	45
Historical average	60	39

➤ Ontario and British Columbia (64%) most likely to say "only for needy."
➤ Quebec least likely to say "only for needy" (54%).
➤ Men (62%) more likely to say "only for needy" than women (57%).
➤ Top income quintile (63%) most likely to say "only for needy."
➤ 45 to 64 years olds most likely to say "only for needy"; youngest adults least likely to say (53%).

Q. Do you believe that only people who have a financial need should be eligible for government benefits such as family allowance or that everyone should receive such benefits?
Source: Decima Research, Decima Quarterly.

Table 43 — Universality of Government Services

	1993 %
The government should not provide services to people who can pay for them out of their own pocket.	52
We can only be sure everyone's needs are met if the government provides the same services to all.	44

➤ Younger Canadians more likely to support universality.

Q. Which view comes closer to your own view?
Source: Carleton University/Institute for Social Research, Canadian National Election Studies.

Table 44 — Free Health Care to All or Needy Only

	Canada %	B.C. %	Winter 1991 Prairies %	Ont. %	Que. %	Atlantic %
All Canadians	74	66	73	78	75	68
Canadians with financial need	25	34	27	21	23	31

➤ Those with university education more likely to say "all Canadians" (80%), as are those in the top income quintile (78%). Younger Canadians more likely to say "all."

Q. *I'm going to name some benefits and services which are or could be funded by governments, and I'd like you to tell me for each one whether you believe that all Canadians should be eligible to receive this benefit, or whether only people who have a financial need should be eligible to receive it? How about free health care?*
Source: Decima Research, Decima Quarterly.

Table 45 — Assessment of Health Care Accessibility in Canada

	Spring 1994 %
Equal access	60
Discriminates on basis of wealth	36

➤ Those with lower income are more likely to say discriminates on the basis of wealth.

Q. *Do you think that all people in Canada have equal access to quality health care or do you think the health care system discriminates on the basis of wealth?*
Source: Insight Canada, Perspectives Canada.

Table 46 — Perceived Importance — Health Care Principle

	1991 Important %	1994 Important %
Universality	93	85
Accessibility	85	77
Portability	89	78
Comprehensiveness	88	73
Public administration	76	63

➤ Those with lower incomes are more likely to say each principle is important.

Q. The Canadian health system is based on five principles developed some years ago. Please tell me how important you think it is to keep each of these five principles: very important, somewhat important, not very important, or not at all important?
Source: Price Waterhouse, The Canada Health Monitor.

Table 47 — Support for User Health Care Fees

	Fall 1992 %
Strongly approve	21
Approve	38
Disapprove	22
Strongly disapprove	18

➤ Quebec most approving of user fees. British Columbia and Atlantic provinces most likely to disapprove.

➤ University-educated, higher income quintiles, older Canadians most likely to approve of user fees.

Q. One method of providing additional funding for health care that has been suggested is charging "user fees." That is, where individuals are charged a small fee every time they use health care services. Generally speaking, do you strongly approve, approve, disapprove or strongly disapprove of charging user fees?
Source: Decima Research, Decima Quarterly.

Table 48 — Attitudes toward Specific Spending Cuts — Fall 1992

	Increase taxes %	Increase deficit %	Cut spending %
Hospital services	31	33	32
Primary and secondary education	30	35	32
Income support for senior citizens	29	38	30
Programs for disabled	29	42	24
Income support for unemployable	26	35	34
Post-secondary education	23	34	39
Children's benefits	23	33	39
Doctors' services	15	20	60
Income support for unemployed	14	28	54

Q.   How about …? Which one of the following three options would you personally choose if this program or service was in financial trouble? Would you increase taxes, increase government spending and the deficit, or cut spending?
Source: Decima Research, Decima Quarterly.

Table 49 — Attitudes toward Specific Spending Cuts among Population Groupings

HOSPITAL SERVICES

	Most likely to say			Least likely to say	
Increase taxes	Increase deficit	Cut spending	Increase taxes	Increase deficit	Cut spending
B.C.	Middle-aged	Quebec	Quebec		B.C.
University		Older	Secondary		Middle income
Middle income		High income	Low income		
Younger		Older	Middle-aged		

POST-SECONDARY EDUCATION

	Most likely to say			Least likely to say	
Increase taxes	Increase deficit	Cut spending	Increase taxes	Increase deficit	Cut spending
B.C.	Quebec	Ontario/Prairies	Quebec	Prairies	B.C./Atlantic
Younger	Younger	Middle-aged	Older		Younger

Table 49 (cont'd.)

CHILDREN'S BENEFITS

	Most likely to say			*Least likely to say*	
Increase taxes	**Increase deficit**	**Cut spending**	**Increase taxes**	**Increase deficit**	**Cut spending**
B.C.	Quebec	Ontario	Quebec	B.C.	Atlantic
Middle income	Elementary	University	Low income	High income	Elementary
	Low income	High income	High income	Middle-aged	Low income
		Middle-aged	Middle-aged		Younger

DOCTORS' SERVICES

	Most likely to say			*Least likely to say*	
Increase taxes	**Increase deficit**	**Cut spending**	**Increase taxes**	**Increase deficit**	**Cut spending**
B.C.	Quebec	Ontario	Quebec	Prairies	B.C.
University	Elementary	Male	Elementary	University	Quebec
					Female
					Elementary

INCOME SUPPORT FOR SENIORS

	Most likely to say			*Least likely to say*	
Increase taxes	**Increase deficit**	**Cut spending**	**Increase taxes**	**Increase deficit**	**Cut spending**
B.C.	Quebec		Quebec	B.C.	Younger
Prairies	Secondary		Secondary		
	Middle-aged				

INCOME SUPPORT FOR UNEMPLOYABLE

	Most likely to say			*Least likely to say*	
Increase taxes	**Increase deficit**	**Cut spending**	**Increase taxes**	**Increase deficit**	**Cut spending**
B.C.	Quebec	Ontario	Quebec	B.C.	Atlantic
	Lower income	Upper income	B.C.	Upper income	Elementary
					Lower income

PRIMARY AND SECONDARY EDUCATION

	Most likely to say			*Least likely to say*	
Increase taxes	**Increase deficit**	**Cut spending**	**Increase taxes**	**Increase deficit**	**Cut spending**
B.C.	Quebec	Ontario	Quebec	Ontario	B.C./Atlantic
University	Elementary		Elementary		
Younger	Younger	Older	Older	Older	Younger

Table 49 (cont'd.)

PROGRAMS FOR THE DISABLED

Most likely to say			Least likely to say		
Increase taxes	Increase deficit	Cut spending	Increase taxes	Increase deficit	Cut spending
B.C.	Quebec		Quebec	Ontario	B.C.
			Prairies		Atlantic

INCOME SUPPORT FOR UNEMPLOYED

Most likely to say			Least likely to say		
Increase taxes	Increase deficit	Cut spending	Increase taxes	Increase deficit	Cut spending
Quebec	B.C./Ontario	B.C.	B.C.	Quebec	Atlantic
Elementary	University		University	Lower income	
Lower income	Elementary		High income	Seniors	
	Higher income				

Table 50 — Post-Secondary Education

	June 1994	
	Agree %	Disagree %
Post-secondary education is an investment, and individual Canadians should take more responsibility for paying for their own education.	68	15
Parents should be responsible for helping their children pay their tuition and living expenses at university or college.	63	19
The cost of university tuition in Canada is already so high that it prevents many students from attending.	59	37
Even if tuition fees were to double, students should pay still more of the actual cost of their education.	50	40

➤ Younger Canadians and those reporting lower household incomes are more likely to express concern about access to post-secondary education.

➤ Alberta and Ontario residents are the most likely to believe students should pay more of the cost of their education.

➤ Quebec residents are easily the most likely to believe that the cost of tuition prevents many students from attending a post-secondary institution.

Q. *I'm going to read you some statements about post-secondary education. I'd like you to tell me if you agree or disagree with each statement using a scale of "1" to "7" where "1" means you strongly disagree and "7" means you strongly agree. A "4" means you neither agree nor disagree. (Agree = 5,6,7/Disagree = 1,2,3)*
Source: *Angus Reid Group*, Social Security Reform Wave II for Human Resources Development Canada.

Table 51 — Views on Pensions

	February 1990 %
All people 65 and older	63
Low income seniors only	35

➤ Younger Canadians are *more* likely to say "all people 65+."

➤ Quebecers more likely to say "low income seniors only" (44%).

Q. Do you think that the old age pension should be paid to all people sixty-five years of age and older, or should it be paid only to low income people sixty-five or older?
Source: Gallup Canada, The Gallup Poll.

Table 52 — Views on Pensions

	1993 %
We can only be sure the needs of all elderly people are met if the government gives pensions to all.	37
The government should not provide pensions to elderly people with above average incomes.	49

➤ Less educated more likely to support universal pensions.

Q. Which view comes closer to your own view?
Source: Carleton University/Institute for Social Research, Canadian National Election Studies.

Table 53 — Old Age Security Benefits

	July 1994 %
We simply cannot afford to supplement the income of seniors who have adequate funds for their retirement.	42
It's unfair to restrict our old age security benefits for those who have contributed to the country throughout their lives.	57

Q. *Which of the following statements comes closer to your own point of view?*
Source: *Ekos Research Associates. Rethinking Government '94.*

Table 54 — Views on Pensions for Those in Need Only

	February 1994 %
Agree	63
Neither agree nor disagree	15
Disagree	23
Mean (1 to 7)	4.83

➤   Quebecers and older Canadians are more likely to agree.

➤   Those earning $70K or more annually are more likely to disagree.

Q. *Over the long term, we must start to target public pensions only to those most in need.*
Source: *Ekos Research Associates, Rethinking Government '94.*

Table 55 — Health Care

	1989 Agree %	1992 Agree %	1994 Agree %
Many people in hospital could be looked after equally well at home. (National)	39	54	71

	1989 Strongly agree %	1992 Strongly agree %	1994 Strongly agree %
Atlantic	n/a	24	n/a
Quebec	n/a	48	n/a
Ontario	n/a	31	n/a
Manitoba/Saskatchewan	n/a	23	n/a
Alberta	n/a	34	n/a
British Columbia	n/a	29	n/a

Q.   Thinking about health care costs, do you strongly agree, somewhat agree, somewhat disagree or strongly disagree with each of the following statements?
Source: Price Waterhouse, The Canada Health Monitor.

Table 56 — Elder Care

April 1994

	Supportive %	Not supportive %
Payments for families who care for an elderly family member	85	15
Additional taxes to support elder care payments	70	28

➤ Support is highest among those with lower household incomes. However, women are no different from men in their levels of support.

Q.   (Exact wording not available.)
Source: Angus Reid Group, The State of the Family in Canada.

Table 57 — Means Test for Social Programs (Family Allowance)

	July 1984 %	July 1985 %
Application of a means test for social programs such as Family Allowance	46	46
Continuing to allow such programs to benefit all Canadians equally	46	47

Q. Are you for...
Source: Goldfarb Consultants, The Goldfarb Report 1985: Book I The State of Affairs in the Nation Today.

Table 58 — Family Allowance

	February 1989 %
Available to all	43
Available only to needy	53
Available to none	2

➤   Quebecers more likely (54%), Ontarians (38%) and British Columbians (37%) least likely to say "available to all."

Q.   Do you believe family allowances should be available to all Canadians, with young children, should they be paid only to those people who need them, or should they be available to none?
Source: Gallup Canada, The Gallup Poll.

Table 59 — Family Allowance

	February 1990 %
All families with children	36
Low income families with children only	62

➤ Younger respondents (18-29) more likely to say "all families with children."

Q. *Do you think that the family allowance should be paid to all families with children, or paid only to low income families with children?*
Source: *Gallup Canada, The Gallup Poll.*

Table 60 — UI Benefits Based on Frequency of Use

	Fall 1994 %
Support lower benefits for frequent UI users	63
Oppose	28

Q. *Would you say that you strongly support, somewhat support, somewhat oppose, or strongly oppose having frequent UI users receive lower benefits or pay higher premiums compared to those who only collect unemployment insurance occasionally?*
Source: *Insight Canada, Perspectives Canada.*

Table 61 — Reforms of Unemployment Insurance

June 1994

	Supportive %	Opposed %
Requiring frequent users of UI to take training or other work related programs in order to quality for UI benefits.	85	15
Reducing the benefits paid after a certain number of claims for frequent UI users.	60	39
Requiring employees with frequent periods of unemployment to pay higher than average insurance premiums while employed.	53	41
Taking household income, or the incomes of everyone in the household, into account when deciding whether someone is eligible for UI benefits and how much they should receive.	50	48

➤ Those from British Columbia were more likely to support taking household income into account when determining UI eligibility.

➤ Respondents from British Columbia and Alberta were more supportive of reducing benefits after a certain number of claims. Those who live in Quebec and the Atlantic regions as well as those earning less than $20K were less likely to support this reform.

Q. I would now like to read to you a series of options for reforming the Unemployment Insurance program. For each, I would like you to tell me whether you would strongly support, somewhat support, somewhat oppose, or strongly oppose each of these options. What about...
Source: Angus Reid Group, Social Security Reform Wave II for Human Resources Development Canada.

Table 62 — Views on Minority Rights

	1993 %
Letting the majority decide	57
Undecided	18
Protecting the needs and rights of minorities	25

➤ Quebecers are most likely to say it is more important to protect the rights of minorities.

➤ Men are more likely to say "let the majority decide," while women are more often undecided.

Q. Which is more important in a democratic society?
Source: Carleton University/Institute for Social Research, Canadian National Election Studies.

Table 63 — Social Services as a Spending Priority

	July 1994 %
Provide job training for 5,000 workers.	74
Provide a $1 million incentive to 10 companies to open a plant in a high unemployment area.	74
Subsidize efforts to reduce violent crime.	69
Buy 4,200 day care places for unemployed single parents so they can look for a job.	67
Fund innovative youth employment counselling services in drop-in centers.	64
Provide start-up funding of $1 million to each of 10 small- and medium-size businesses in the high technology and information industry.	64
Reduce the annual deficit by $10 million.	63
Create about 500 partially subsidized jobs.	63
Decrease taxes by $10 million.	56
Fund a pre-natal program to reduce the incidence of newborns at risk because of their small weight.	52
Fund a citizenship learning program for young Canadians.	48
Hire 100 new officers to increase control of illegal immigration.	
Support 10 festivals that encourage tourism.	42
Develop a 1-800 "how to" hot line providing information on training.	42
Set up a system to get public input on important government decisions through electronic means.	41
Hold 10 top-level conferences between governments, business, labour and representatives of citizen groups to come up with solutions to one problem.	40
Maintain the regional CBC news broadcast in two cities near you.	
Help 2,500 immigrants learn one of the official languages.	32
Provide $10 million in assistance to a developing country to improve their industrial infrastructure.	31
Provide subsidies to maintain the existence of 50 professional theatre and dance companies.	24
Create a youth travel exchange program to allow 10,000 kids to spend a week in a community in another province.	30
Fund the adoption by Canadians of a village in Ethiopia to encourage sustainable development.	29
Assist Canadian publishers in producing 200 books that would not be otherwise commercially viable.	23

Q.   *Which of the following two 10 million $ alternatives would you chose in the best public interest?*
Source: *Ekos Research Associates*. Rethinking Government '94.

Table 64 — Views on Provincial Transfers

	August 1988 %	August 1989 %	August 1990 %
Increase	60	58	58
Stay the same	24	28	28
Decrease	5	5	6
Be eliminated	3	2	4

➤ Those in the Atlantic provinces are slightly more likely to say "increased."

Q.   *Do you believe that federal government spending on poorer regions in Canada should increase, remain the same, decrease or be eliminated?*
Source: *Gallup Canada, The Gallup Poll.*

Table 65 — Support for Provincial Transfers

	March 1972 %
Approve	73
Disapprove	13
Undecided	14

➤ Those with more education more likely to approve.

➤ Atlantic Canadians more likely to approve; British Columbians and Albertans more likely to disapprove.

Q.   *As you may know, the federal government has developed a programme whereby financial assistance is given to the "have not" provinces, that is, those with a smaller population or less industry than say, Ontario, Alberta and B.C. In general, do you approve or disapprove of this programme?*
Source: *Gallup Canada, The Gallup Poll.*

Table 66 — Views on Regional Unemployment Assistance

	August 1988 %	August 1989 %	August 1990 %
Financial assistance to those who wish to stay at home	52	44	50
Encourage unemployed to move	33	33	31
Do not get involved in these matters	11	17	15

> Those with lower household incomes more likely to say "financial assistance"; higher household incomes more likely to say "encourage to move."

> Newfoundlanders and Quebecers more likely to say "financial assistance"; Westerners and Ontarians more likely to say "encourage to move."

Q. *Do you believe that the federal government should give financial assistance to unemployed people in Canada's poorer regions who wish to stay in their home area, encourage them to move to a more prosperous region, or not become involved in such matters?*
Source: Gallup Canada, The Gallup Poll.

Table 67 — Views on Immigration

	Summer 1994 %
Too many	51
The right number	36
Too few	8

> Education is strongly correlated with those having less education more likely to say there are too many immigrants.

> Quebecers are the least likely to say there are too many immigrants and the most likely to say too few or about the right amount.

Q. *I'm now going to ask you a few questions about immigration. In your opinion, do you feel that there are too many, too few or about the right number of immigrants coming to Canada?*
Source: Insight Canada, Perspectives Canada.

Table 68 — Views on Immigration

	August 1989 %	February 1994 %
Increase	14	14
Keep at current level	47	33
Decrease	33	51

Q. (1989) *If it were your job to plan an immigration policy for Canada at this time, would you be inclined to increase immigration, decrease immigration or keep the number of immigrants at about the current level?*
Source: Gallup Canada, The Gallup Poll.
Q. (1994) *If it were your job to plan the government's immigration policy for the future, 10 years from now, how many immigrants do you think should be allowed to come to Canada every year? Please use a 7-point scale where 1 means much less than now, 7 means much more than now and the midpoint 4 means about the same as now.*
Source: Ekos Research Associates, Rethinking Government '94.

Table 69 — Views on Immigration

	Summer 1994	
	Most new immigrants to Canada respect and cherish the same principles and values as I do. %	Immigrants create more jobs than they take away from people who were born in Canada. %
Disagree	34	34
Neither agree nor disagree	28	34
Agree	36	29
Mean	3.00	2.89

➤ Older Canadians are more likely to agree that immigrants cherish the same principles as they do.

➤ Immigrants and first-generation Canadians are the most likely to agree that immigrants create more jobs than they take away.

➤ British Columbians and Prairie residents are the most likely to agree that immigrants create more jobs than they take away.

Q. *I'd like you to rate the following statements about immigration, using a scale of one to five, where one is disagree strongly, five is agree strongly, and three means you neither agree nor disagree …*
Source: Insight Canada, Perspectives Canada.

Table 70 — Views on Immigration

	November 1993 %	February 1995 %
Provides a good balance of people and backgrounds coming to Canada.	54	46
Allows too many people of different races and cultures into Canada.	41	46

➤ Younger Canadians, the university-educated, those of minority ethnic origins, Atlantic Canadians and those living in the Prairie provinces are most likely to say current policy provides "a good balance." Seniors and those living in British Columbia and Quebec are most like to say current policy allows too many different races and cultures in.

Q. In your personal opinion, how would you describe Canada's immigration policy?
Source: Decima Research, A Research Report to the Canadian Council of Christians and Jews.

Table 71 — Views on Multiculturalism

	February/July 1994 Mean (1 to 7)
A mixture of different lifestyles and cultures makes Canada a more attractive place to live.	5.40
One of the best sources of our Canadian identity is the fact that we are a nation of immigrants.	4.67
I worry that the traditional Canadian way of life is being threatened by high levels of immigration.	4.23
Sometimes, I wish we could turn back the clock and return to the "old Canada" of 25 years ago.	4.05

➤ B.C. residents and those with university education are more likely to agree with first statement.
➤ Quebecers are less likely to agree with second statement. Ontario, B.C. residents and older Canadians are more likely to agree.
➤ Residents of Ontario, older Canadians, those earning $20K - $30K annually and those with high-school or less education are more likely to agree with third statement. Younger Canadians (16-24 years), those with university education and those earning $70K or more per year are less likely to agree.
➤ Older Canadians (45 years plus) and those with high-school or less education are more likely to agree with fourth statement. Younger Canadians (16-24) and those with university education are less likely to agree.

Q. Now I'm going to read you a few statements. Please tell me how much you agree or disagree with each of them. Please use a 7-point scale where 1 is strongly disagree, 7 is strongly agree and the midpoint 4 is neither agree nor disagree.
Source: Ekos Research Associates, Rethinking Government '94.

Table 72 — Views on Multiculturalism

June/July 1991

➤ 77% believe multiculturalism will enrich Canada's culture.

➤ 73% believe multiculturalism ensures that people from various cultural backgrounds will have a sense of belonging to Canada.

➤ 73% believe multiculturalism will provide greater equality of opportunity for all groups.

➤ 37% believe that multiculturalism will create greater conflict between groups.

➤ 26% believe that multiculturalism will force Canada to change too quickly.

Source: *Angus Reid, Survey conducted by the Angus Reid Group for Multiculturalism and Citizenship Canada.*

Table 73 — Views on Multiculturalism

Multiculturalism will...	June/July 1974 % agreeing	June/July 1991 % agreeing
destroy the Canadian way of life	32	18
enrich Canadian culture	61	78
cause greater conflict between groups of different origins	37	37

Source: *Angus Reid, Survey conducted by the Angus Reid Group for Multiculturalism and Citizenship Canada. Cautionary note: "Comparisons between 1974 and 1991 must be interpreted with caution due to changes in the wording and ordering of questions, the context within which questions were asked and differences in the demographic characteristics and the sizes of the samples."*

Table 74 — Vision of Multicultural Society

| | March-August 1987 | |
	General public %	Elites %
To keep to themselves as much as possible	1	1
Neither	5	5
To live and work together so that they can learn to understand each other	92	94

Q. *In general, it's better for people of different races:*
Source: *Institute for Social Research*, Attitudes toward Civil Liberties and the Canadian Charter of Rights.

Table 75 — Views on Pluralism and Community

| | February 1995 | |
	Ideal %	Actual %
A society where members of the community share the same language, race and religion.	8	6
A society where members of the community observe different religions and come from different racial or ethnic backgrounds, but who share a common way of life and common values.	74	49
A society where members of the community observe different religions and come from different racial and ethnic backgrounds, and who each follow a way of life particular to their religion or race.	17	43

➤ Seniors, those with less formal education, Quebecers and those living in large cities are most likely to say they prefer a "homogeneous" society.

➤ Younger Canadians, those with lower SES, rural Canadians and those of minority ethnicities, as well as Atlantic Canadians, are most likely to say they prefer a society that is diverse and where groups follow their distinct ways of life.

Q. *Community means different things to different people. Which of the following best describes your idea of an ideal community?*
Q. *And, which of these BEST describes Canada today?*
Source: *Decima Research*, A Research Report to the Canadian Council of Christians and Jews.

Table 76 — Views on Multiculturalism

	February 1995 Mean (1 to 7)
Where there is a conflict between the traditions of ethnic minorities and the Canadian way of life, the Canadian way of life should always come first.	5.16
Being a multicultural society is one of the things I like best about Canada.	5.10

Q. I'm going to read you a list of statements various people have made at one time or another. Please tell me how you personally feel about each statement by giving me a number between 1 and 7, where "1" means you "totally disagree" with the statement and "7" means you "totally agree" with the statement. Many people's opinions fall somewhere in between these two points depending on how they feel about the statement.

Source: Decima Research, A Research Report to the Canadian Council of Christians and Jews.

Table 77 — Melting Pot versus Mosaic

	February 1995 %
It is the right of every individual in Canada to follow their own ethnic traditions, even if these traditions conflict with the values of the Canadian majority.	25
The values of the Canadian majority should take precedence over minority traditions when there is a conflict.	72

➤ Seniors, those of British/Irish ancestry, and those from British Columbia are most likely to agree that the majority should take precedence. Younger Canadians, those of minority ethnic ancestry, and those from Atlantic Canada are least likely to agree that the majority should take precedence.

Q. Which view is closest to your own?

Source: Decima Research, A Research Report to the Canadian Council of Christians and Jews.

Table 78 — Melting Pot versus Mosaic

	November 1993 %	February 1995 %
Different ethnic groups should try to adapt to the value system and way of life of the majority in Canadian society.	72	77
Different ethnic groups should maintain their differences and not have to adapt to the value system and way of life of the majority in Canadian society.	23	18

➤ Seniors more likely to support an "assimilationist" view, as are those with less education, and those of British/Irish ancestry, as well as those from British Columbia and the Prairie provinces.

Q. *Thinking of these two points of view, which view is closest to your own?*
Source: Decima Research, A Research Report to the Canadian Council of Christians and Jews.

Table 79 — Melting Pot versus Mosaic

	March-August 1987	
	General public %	Elites %
Basically agree	63	43
Basically disagree	35	54

➤ Quebecers are particularly likely to agree.

➤ Those of lower SES and seniors are more likely to agree.

➤ Immigrants do not differ from native-born Canadians in their attitudes.

Q. *People who come to live in Canada should try harder to be more like other Canadians.*
Source: Institute for Social Research, Attitudes toward Civil Liberties and the Canadian Charter of Rights.

Table 80 — Melting Pot versus Mosaic

	March-August 1987	
	General public %	Elites %
Strongly agree	32	22
Agree	43	47
Disagree	19	25
Strongly disagree	3	4

➤ Those of lower SES and seniors are more likely to agree.

Q. While it is all well and good to celebrate one's heritage, it is more important for new immigrants to learn what it is to be Canadian than to cling to their old ways.
Source: Institute for Social Research, Attitudes toward Civil Liberties and the Canadian Charter of Rights.

Table 81 — Tolerance for Minority Cultures

	June/July 1974 % agreeing	June/July 1991 % agreeing
Immigrants should forget cultural backgrounds as soon as possible.	28	32
Ethnic groups should keep their culture to themselves.	51	39
The unity of the country is threatened by ethnic groups sticking to their old ways.	36	42
People coming to the country should change their behaviour to be more like Canadians.	56	46

Source: Angus Reid, Survey conducted by the Angus Reid Group for Multiculturalism and Citizenship Canada. Cautionary note: "Comparisons between 1974 and 1991 must be interpreted with caution due to changes in the wording and ordering of questions, the context within which questions were asked and differences in the demographic characteristics and the sizes of the samples."

Table 82 — Support for Multiculturalism Funding

	February 1995 %
Increased	8
Remain at the same level	43
Decreased	45

➤ Those most supportive of multiculturalism policy, and most likely to suggest that spending should be increased, include younger Canadians, those with university education, and those who live in medium- or large-sized cities, as well as those of minority ethnicities. Atlantic Canadians are most supportive of multiculturalism policy.

➤ Seniors, those with less formal education, those living in small cities and rural areas, and Westerners are least supportive.

Q. *At the present time, the federal government spends approximately $25 million on funding multicultural groups. Do you feel this level of funding should be increased, decreased, or should it remain at this level?*
Source: *Decima Research*, A Research Report to the Canadian Council of Christians and Jews.

Table 83 — Support for Multicultural Policy

	June/July 1974 % agreeing	June/July 1991 % agreeing
Government should support activities aimed at preserving cultural heritages	69	58

Source: *Angus Reid, Survey conducted by the Angus Reid Group for Multiculturalism and Citizenship Canada. Cautionary note: "Comparisons between 1974 and 1991 must be interpreted with caution due to changes in the wording and ordering of questions, the context within which questions were asked and differences in the demographic characteristics and the sizes of the samples."*

Table 84 — Support for Multiculturalism

	February 1995 %
Strongly support	10
Somewhat support	45
Neither support nor oppose	12
Somewhat oppose	19
Strongly oppose	8

Q.   *And, overall, do you strongly support, somewhat support, somewhat oppose, or strongly oppose the federal government's current multiculturalism policy?*
Source: *Decima Research*, A Research Report to the Canadian Council of Christian and Jews.

Table 85 — Support for Multiculturalism Policy

	August 1991* % support	February 1995** % support
Recognizing that cultural and racial diversity is a fundamental characteristic of Canadian society.	76	63
Ensuring that organizations and institutions reflect and respect the cultural and racial diversity of Canadians.	79	66
Developing materials for all school systems in Canada to teach children and teachers about other cultures and ways of life.	80	66
Funding festivals and special events celebrating different cultures.	58	41
Ensuring equal access to jobs regardless of ethnic or racial background.	90	78
Help Canadian citizens who are immigrants to acquire the knowledge and skills they need to integrate into Canadian society.	85	76

➤   Those of minority ethnic origin are consistently supportive of each element of multiculturalism policy, and those of British, Irish, European origin are the least supportive.

➤   Those living in larger cities are consistently more supportive, as are British Columbians. The suggestion is that exposure to diversity may enhance the view that state intervention is needed to protect minorities.

Q.   *I'd like to read you some possible elements of federal multiculturalism policy. For each element, I'd like you to tell me if you support or oppose it. Please indicate your opinion on a scale of 1 to 7, where "1" means you "totally oppose" the policy, and "7" means you "totally support" this part of the policy. A neutral answer would be "4."*
* Source: *Angus Reid Group*, Multiculturalism National Study.
** Source: *Decima Research*, A Research Report to the Canadian Council of Christians and Jews.

Table 86 — Tolerance for Minority Cultures

	March-August 1987	
	General public %	Elites %
Basically agree	71	50
Basically disagree	26	48

➤ Seniors are more likely to agree. Interestingly, those who are not born in Canada are as likely to agree as those born in Canada.

Q. *Immigrants often bring discrimination upon themselves by their own personal attitudes and habits.*
Source: Institute for Social Research, Attitudes toward Civil Liberties and the Canadian Charter of Rights.

Table 87 — Tolerance for Minority Cultures

	March-August 1987	
	General public %	Elites %
Mainly agree	39	24
Mainly disagree	48	66

➤ Seniors are more likely to agree.

Q. *If minority groups hope to be liked better, they should try first to get rid of their harmful and irritating habits.*
Source: Institute for Social Research, Attitudes toward Civil Liberties and the Canadian Charter of Rights.

Table 88 — Tolerance for Minority Cultures

| | March-August 1987 | |
	General public %	Elites %
Mainly agree	35	23
Mainly disagree	52	68

➤ Those with less education, and less income, and seniors, are more likely to agree.

Q. *The trouble with letting certain minority groups into a nice neighbourhood is that they gradually give it their own atmosphere.*
Source: *Institute for Social Research*, Attitudes toward Civil Liberties and the Canadian Charter of Rights.

Table 89 — Support for Anti-Hate Laws

| | March-August 1987 | |
	General public %	Elites %
Yes, should be against law	72	78
No, should not be against law	25	20

| | Feel differently if results in less freedom of speech? | | Feel differently if results in more prejudice? | |
	General public %	Elites %	General public %	Elites %
Yes, feel differently	46	36	40	38
No, feel same	48	61	54	58

Q. *Do you think it should be against the law to write or speak in a way that promotes hatred toward a particular racial or religious group?*
Q. *(Among those who say "yes, should be against law.") If this results in less freedom of speech about important public issues, would you feel differently about it being against the law?*
Q. *(Among those who say "no, should not be against law.") If this results in more racial and religious prejudice, would you feel differently about it NOT being against the law?*
Source: *Institute for Social Research*, Attitudes toward Civil Liberties and the Canadian Charter of Rights.

Table 90 — Views on Equality

	March-August 1987	
	General public %	Elites %
Mainly agree	24	12
Mainly disagree	73	83

➤ Those with less education, seniors and those with lower incomes are more likely to agree.

Q. *Just as it is true of a fine race horse, some breeds of people are just naturally better than others.*
Source: *Institute for Social Research*, Attitudes toward Civil Liberties and the Canadian Charter of Rights.

Table 91 — Views on Equality

	March-August 1987	
	General public %	Elites %
Mainly agree	39	32
Mainly disagree	55	62

➤ Those with less education and seniors are more likely to agree.

Q. *We have to teach children that all men are created equal, but almost everyone knows that some are better than others.*
Source: *Institute for Social Research*, Attitudes toward Civil Liberties and the Canadian Charter of Rights.

Table 92 — Views on Racial Equality

| | March-August 1987 | |
	General public %	Elites %
Mainly agree	30	17
Mainly disagree	57	75

➤ Those with lower incomes and less education, as well as seniors, are more likely to agree.

Q. *When it comes to the things that count most, all races are certainly not equal.*
Source: Institute for Social Research, Attitudes toward Civil Liberties and the Canadian Charter of Rights.

Table 93 — Views on Equality

| | 1987* | | 1993** |
	General public %	Elites %	General public %
No matter how we treat everyone, some people will turn out better than others.	64	76	70
Neither	5	7	5
If we really gave every person an equal chance, almost all of them would turn out to be equally worthwhile.	28	15	25

➤ Women, those with lower incomes and younger Canadians are more likely to believe that, if given an equal chance, all would turn out equal.

Q. *Which of these opinions about equality comes closer to what you believe?*
*Source: Institute for Social Research, Attitudes toward Civil Liberties and the Canadian Charter of Rights.
** Source: Carleton University/Institute for Social Research, Canadian National Election Studies.

Table 94 — Ideal Society

	March-August 1987	
	General public %	Elites %
All people should earn about the same	12	5
Neither	13	20
People with more ability should earn higher salaries	71	73

➤ Those born outside of Canada, seniors, those earning more income and men, are more likely to believe that people with more ability should earn higher salaries.

Q.   *In a fair economic system:*
Source: *Institute for Social Research*, Attitudes Toward Civil Liberties and the Canadian Charter of Rights.

Table 95 — Reasons for Wealth

	March-August 1987	
	General public %	Elites %
Have usually done so at the expense of other people	13	10
Neither	16	32
Are proof of what you get if you are willing to work and take advantage of the opportunities all of us have.	65	55

➤ Those with less income are more likely to say the wealthy have achieved at the expense of others.

Q.   *People who have made a lot of money:*
Source: *Institute for Social Research*, Attitudes toward Civil Liberties and the Canadian Charter of Rights.

Table 96 — Responsibility for Personal Success

| | 1993 | |
	Agree %	Disagree %
Most people who don't get ahead should not blame the system; they have only themselves to blame.	52	45
If people work hard they almost always get what they want.	63	36
The welfare state makes people nowadays less willing to look after themselves.	78	19

➤ Men are more individualistic, and more likely to believe the welfare state leads to dependency.

➤ Those over 65 years were more likely to agree with the first statement.

➤ Respondents from the Atlantic region were less likely to agree with the first statement.

➤ Quebecers more likely to agree with second statement.

➤ Quebecers less likely to agree with third statement.

Q. For each statement below, please indicate if you strongly agree, agree, disagree, or strongly disagree by writing the number that best represents how you feel in the space at the right of each statement.
Source: Carleton University/Institute for Social Research, Canadian National Election Studies.

Table 97 — Perception of Racism

	November 1993 %	February 1995 %
Great deal of racism	25	25
Some racism	61	60
Not very much racism	12	13
No racism at all	3	2

Q. In your view, to what extent does racism exist in Canada? By racism I mean the existence of attitudes or actions that lead to discrimination against individuals or groups on the basis of their race or ethnic group background. Would you say there is a great deal, some, not very much, or no racism at all?
Source: Decima Research, A Research Report to the Canadian Council of Christians and Jews.

Table 98 — Perception of Racism

	November 1993 %	February 1995 %
Very serious	14	13
Somewhat serious	60	57
Not very serious	24	27
Not at all serious	2	2

➤ Racism is perceived to be particularly problematic in Quebec, among younger Canadians, and among lower socioeconomic status groups. Those of minority ethnicities are also more likely to perceive a problem.

Q. *How serious a problem do you think racism is today in Canada?*
Source: *Decima Research*, A Research Report to the Canadian Council of Christians and Jews.

Table 99 — Views on Equality

	March-August 1987	
	General public %	Elites %
Agree	69	55
Disagree	28	42

➤ Those with less education and less income are more likely to agree.

Q. *If people were treated more equally in this country, we would have many fewer problems.*
Source: *Institute for Social Research*, Attitudes toward Civil Liberties and the Canadian Charter of Rights.

Table 100 — Views on Equality

| | 1987* | | 1993** |
	General public %	Elites %	General public %
Agree	30	18	47
Disagree	68	81	48

➤ Those with less education and seniors are more likely to agree.

Q. *We have gone too far in pushing equal rights in this country.*
* *Source: Institute for Social Research,* Attitudes toward Civil Liberties and the Canadian Charter of Rights.
** *Source: Carleton University/Institute for Social Research,* Canadian National Election Studies.

Table 101 — Perceptions of Equal Opportunity

| | 1987* | | 1993** |
	General public %	Elites %	General public %
Agree	56	34	40
Disagree	42	65	59

➤ Those with less education and less income, as well as Quebecers are most likely to agree.

Q.   *One of the big problems in this country is that we don't give everyone an equal chance. Do you basically agree or basically disagree with that statement?*
* *Source: Institute for Social Research,* Attitudes toward Civil Liberties and the Canadian Charter of Rights.
** *Source: Carleton University/Institute for Social Research,* Canadian National Election Studies.

Table 102 — Importance of Gender Equality

| | March-August 1987 | |
	General public %	Elites %
Very important	72	75
Somewhat important	23	20
Not important	5	3

➤ Those earning higher incomes are more likely to say "very" important. Men and women do not differ. Younger Canadians are also more likely to say "very" important.

Q. How important is it to guarantee equality between men and women in all aspects of life?
Source: Institute for Social Research, Attitudes toward Civil Liberties and the Canadian Charter of Rights.

Table 103 — Guaranteeing Equality for Women

| | March-August 1987 | |
	General public %	Elites %
Yes, should have quotas	31	31
No, should not have quotas	66	66

➤ Those with lower household incomes are more supportive of quotas, as are women.
➤ Quotas are most strongly supported in Quebec and the Atlantic provinces and most weakly supported in the West.

| | Feel same if not hire best person? | | Feel same if women remain unequal? | |
	General public %	Elites %	General public %	Elites %
Yes, feel same	31	50	48	55
No, feel differently	65	47	48	39

Q. Do you think large companies should have quotas to ensure a fixed percentage of women are hired or should women get no special treatment?
Q. (Asked of those who say "should have quotas.") Would you feel the same even if this means not hiring the best person for the job?
Q. (Asked of those who say "no special treatment.") Would you feel the same even if it means that women remain economically unequal?
Source: Institute for Social Research, Attitudes toward Civil Liberties and the Canadian Charter of Rights.

Table 104 — Attitudes Toward Job Quotas

	1993 %
Quotas should be used to increase the number of women in good jobs	7
Undecided	8
Hiring should be based strictly on merit	84

➤ Quebecers feel less affinity toward hiring based on merit.

Q.   When it comes to job hiring:
Source: Carleton University/Institute for Social Research, Canadian National Election Studies.

Table 105 — Perception of a Prejudice Problem

June/July, 1991

➤ 74% believe that people should make it on their own and not blame racial/cultural backgrounds for problems.

➤ Still, 68% believe that problems with racism and prejudice will not solve themselves over time without government intervention.

➤ Only 30% believe that hiring certain groups of people is an employer's own business.

➤ 66% believe that discrimination against non-whites is a problem in Canada.

➤ 56% believe that it is more difficult for non-whites to be successful than whites.

➤ 54% also believe that society as a whole discriminates against some whites.

Source: Angus Reid, Survey conducted by the Angus Reid Group for Multiculturalism and Citizenship Canada.

Table 106 — Assessments of Charities' Contribution

	October 1987 %
Very positive	35
Somewhat positive	56
Not too positive	8
Not at all positive	0

➤ Quebecers are less positive, except for Quebecers of high SES.

➤ Women outside of Quebec and the religious tend to be more positive.

Q. And would you say that charities and non-profit organizations generally make a very positive, somewhat positive, not too positive, or not at all positive contribution to the community?
Source: Decima Research, Nationwide Survey of Attitudes toward Philanthropy for the Canadian Centre for Philanthropy.

Table 107 — Government versus Third Sector Responsibility

	October 1987 Mean (-5 to +5)
The work that charitable and non-profit organizations do should not be a substitute for government's responsibility to provide services for the public.	2.52
I believe that if Canadians would give more money to charitable and non-profit organizations, then we wouldn't have to rely on government as much to do things.	0.76

Q. I'm going to read you a series of statements various people have made. I'd like you to tell me how you personally feel about each statement by giving me a number between -5 and +5, where -5 means you totally disagree with the statement and +5 means you totally agree with the statement. Many people's opinions fall somewhere in between these two points depending on how they feel about the statement. The first statement is…
Source: Decima Research, Nationwide Survey of Attitudes toward Philanthropy for the Canadian Centre for Philanthropy.

Table 108 — Views on Canadian Generosity

	February 1994 Mean (1 to 7)
One of the best things about Canada and Canadians is that we are generous and prepared to help people in need.	5.70
One of the biggest myths about Canada and Canadians is that we are generous and prepared to help people in need.	4.35

➤ No regional or other demographic variances for first statement.

➤ Quebecers, older Canadians, and those earning less than $20K annually are more likely to agree with second statement.

➤ Residents of British Columbia and those with university education less likely to agree with second statement.

Q. Now I am going to read you some more statements. Please rate the degree to which you agree or disagree with these statements using a 7-point scale where 1 means you strongly disagree, 7 means you strongly agree and the midpoint 4 means you neither agree nor disagree.
Source: Ekos Research Associates, Rethinking Government '94.

Table 109 — Views on Sector Responsibilities

	October 1987	
	Has the most responsibility now %	Should have the most responsibility %
The general public	56	40
Businesses	21	20
Foundations	12	7
Government	11	32

➤ Those who believe that government should have the most responsibility to fund the charitable sector include women, younger Canadians and seniors, those with less education, and those with lower incomes, along with they are less likely to give personal charitable donations.

Q. And, from your point of view, which of these groups should be the most responsible for providing funds to charitable and non-profit organizations?
Source: Decima Research, Nationwide Survey of Attitudes toward Philanthropy for the Canadian Centre for Philanthropy.

Table 110 — Attitudes Toward Philanthropy

	October 1987 Mean (-5 to +5)
It's important to give to the community because you never know when you might need help yourself.	3.08
If more people were generous with their time and money, we could meet a lot more of our community's needs.	2.92
Giving back to the community through donations to charitable and other non-profit organizations is one of the most important things you can do.	2.33
I'd like to see Canadians double the amount of money they donate to charitable and other non-profit organizations over the next five years.	1.22
There's a new generation of Canadians who are more caring and compassionate for people than the previous generation.	-0.48
Individual Canadians tend to be less generous in their giving to charities and other non-profit organizations than Americans.	-0.91
I believe that you should give until it hurts.	-2.33

Q.   *I'm going to read you a series of statements various people have made. I'd like you to tell me how you personally feel about each statement by giving me a number between -5 and +5, where -5 means you totally disagree with the statement and +5 means you totally agree with the statement. Many people's opinions fall somewhere in between these two points depending on how they feel about the statement. The first statement is…*
Source: *Decima Research, Nationwide Survey of Attitudes toward Philanthropy for the Canadian Centre for Philanthropy.*

Table 111 — Assessments of Generosity

	October 1987 %
Very generous	12
Somewhat generous	56
Not too generous	29
Not at all generous	3

Q.   *From your own experience, do you think people are mostly very generous, somewhat generous, not too generous or not at all generous in their contributions to charitable and non-profit organizations.*
Source: *Decima Research, Nationwide Survey of Attitudes toward Philanthropy for the Canadian Centre for Philanthropy.*

Table 112 — *Likelihood of Donating Time*

	October 1987 %
Very likely	25
Somewhat likely	38
Somewhat unlikely	19
Very unlikely	18

➤ Those most likely to consider volunteering are women, those aged between 30 and 60 years, the employed and better educated, women employed in part-time jobs, those who are married or formerly married, those living in households with children, and residents of the Atlantic provinces.

➤ The majority of Canadians are more likely to say they would rather donate money than volunteer their time.

Q. *Thinking about all the things you might do in your spare time, how likely are you to consider volunteering your time to charity or non-profit organizations? Would you say you are very likely, somewhat likely, somewhat unlikely or very unlikely to consider volunteering some of your spare time in this way?*
Source: *Decima Research, Nationwide Survey of Attitudes toward Philanthropy for the Canadian Centre of Philanthropy.*

Table 113 — *Reasons for Non-Donation*

	October 1987 %
No funds available	40
Never been approached	21
Charities fraudulent	13
Never think about it	9
Other	12

Q. *What was your main reason for not donating?*
Source: *Decima Research, Nationwide Survey of Attitudes toward Philanthropy for the Canadian Centre for Philanthropy.*

Table 114 — Effect of Taxation on Generosity

	July 1994 %
Agree	79
Neither agree nor disagree	16
Disagree	15
Mean (1 to 7)	5.21

➤ Quebecers and younger Canadians (16-24 years) are less likely to agree.

Q. High taxes are reducing Canadians' compassion for those people in need.
Source: Ekos Research Associates, Rethinking Government '94.

Table 115 — Importance of Third Sector Work

	October 1987 Mean (1 to 10)
Seeking cures for disabling or fatal diseases	8.39
Providing assistance to the disadvantaged in the community	7.85
Supporting hospitals and health care services	7.78
Promoting conservation of the environment	7.38
Supporting post-secondary education	6.44
Promoting amateur sports and fitness	6.38
Supporting projects in Third World countries	6.15
Promoting social causes	6.07
Helping to meet spiritual and religious needs	5.82
Supporting arts and culture	5.28

Q. For each of the following could you tell me, using a 10-point scale, when "1" means not at all important and "10" means extremely important, how important is the work that charitable or non-profit organizations do in each area?
Source: Decima Research, Nationwide Survey of Attitudes toward Philanthropy for the Canadian Centre for Philanthropy.

Table 116 — Views on Private Sector Role in Public Services

	July 1994 %
Agree	69
Neither agree nor disagree	19
Disagree	11
Mean (1 to 7)	4.58

➤ No regional or other demographic variances for this statement.

Q.   When it comes to providing public services to Canadians, I think that the private sector should have a much larger role.
Source: Ekos Research Associates, Rethinking Government '94.

Table 117 — Responsibility of the Private Sector

	Spring 1992 %
Major responsibility	36
Minor responsibility	53
No real responsibility	11

➤ Quebec more likely to say "major responsibility." British Columbia most likely to say "no responsibility."
➤ Lower income more likely to say "major responsibility." Top income quintile more likely to say "no responsibility."

Q.   Some people say that the private sector should play a major role in helping the poor, because the business community has the expertise and financial resources to provide the kind of opportunities that will help people to pull themselves out of poverty. In your opinion, does the private sector have a major responsibility, a minor responsibility or no real responsibility to provide this kind of assistance to the poor?
Source: Decima Research, Decima Quarterly.

Table 118 — Responsibility of the Private Sector

	Fall 1990 %
Shift responsibility to private sector	21
Government should continue to provide	75

➤ Prairies (25%) most likely to say shift to private sector. Atlantic Canadians least likely (18%).

➤ Older Canadians most likely to say shift to private sector.

Q. Some people say that the only way to permanently solve our deficit and government spending problems is to shift responsibility for social programs like pensions and child care to the private sector and to force business to assume responsibility for providing them. Other people say that government must continue to provide pensions and new programs like child care because it is the only way to ensure that all Canadians are protected and have access to these sorts of programs. Which view is closest to your own?
Source: Decima Research, Decima Quarterly.

Table 119 — Trust in the Private Sector

	Jan. 1983	Jan. 1984	July 1984	Jan. 1985	July 1985
Corporations operating in Canada make...					
Too much money	39	40	39	38	44
About the right amount	44	43	43	46	44
Not enough	15	13	12	12	8

Source: Goldfarb Consultants, The Goldfarb Report 1985: Book I The State of Affairs in the Nation Today.

Table 120 — Faith in Private Enterprise

	1993 % agreeing
Under the private enterprise system, working people do not get their fair share of what they produce.	41
When businesses are allowed to make as much money as they can, everyone profits in the long run, including the poor.	32

➤ Atlantic Canadians are most likely to agree that working people do not get their fair share; British Columbians are least likely.

➤ Those with less education are also most likely to agree working people do not get their fair share.

Q. For each statement below, please indicate if you strongly agree, agree, disagree, or strongly disagree by writing the number that best represents how you feel in the space at the right of each statement.
Source: Carleton University/Institute for Social Research, Canadian National Election Studies.

Table 121 — Faith in the Public Sector

	Jan. 1983	Jan. 1984	July 1984	Jan. 1985	July 1985
			% of respondents		
Preferred Approach to Increasing Economic Activity					
Less taxation of industry leaving more funds with industry to invest	65	66	65	62	59
More taxation of industry and redistribution of funds	31	31	28	34	39
Federal Government Should Move More Toward...					
More direct intervention in and control of the free market system	36	34	29	35	34
Less direct intervention in the system	60	62	63	60	60
Free Market System is Working Worse Than It Used To	51	35	n/a	28	23

Source: Goldfarb Consultants, The Goldfarb Report 1985: Book I The State of Affairs in the Nation Today.

Table 122 — *Perceived Effectiveness in the Economy*

	1993	
	% agreeing	**% disagreeing**
Governments cannot do much to solve our economic problems	28	70

➤ Older Canadians are more likely to agree that the government can do little to solve our economic problems.

Q.   Could you tell me if you strongly agree, somewhat agree, somewhat disagree or strongly disagree with the following statements?
Source: Carleton University/Institute for Social Research, Canadian National Election Studies.

Table 123 — *Perceived Influence of Federal Government*

	Summer 1994			
	A lot of influence	**Some influence**	**Little influence**	**No influence at all**
	%	%	%	%
The overall state of the economy	51	31	13	3
The state of the environment	51	30	14	3
National unity	45	29	17	4
The level of unemployment	43	33	17	4
Keeping Quebec in Canada	39	31	20	7
The number of poor and homeless	39	33	19	5
The amount of crime	33	32	25	7
The level of prejudice/discrimination	27	31	26	12

➤ On the whole, immigrants and first-generation Canadians are more likely than other Canadians to believe the federal government can have influence.
➤ Quebecers are also consistently less likely to believe the federal government can have influence.
➤ On the issues of the poor, crime and racial discrimination, older Canadians are more likely to believe the federal government can have influence.
➤ The issue of the environment stands out in that Ontarians, those who live in urban communities, and those with more education are more likely to believe the government can have influence.

Q.   I'd like to ask you now about the influence the federal government can have over the state of affairs in Canada. For each of the following issues, I'd like you to tell me whether the federal government can have a lot of influence, some influence, little influence, or no influence at all. How about...
Source: Insight Canada, Perspectives Canada.

Table 124 — *Perceived Effectiveness of Government Programs*

	February 1994 Mean (1 to 7)
Too many government programs just don't work.	5.30
Canadian government no longer works and needs major changes.	4.96
Canadian aid to the poor in the Third World doesn't help because it is poorly managed by officials in Ottawa.	4.61
When I think of the severity of social problems like violence, poverty and disease, it's hard to believe government can really make any difference.	3.67
I don't think the federal government can really influence our economic future.	3.38

➤ Younger Canadians (16-24 years) and those earning less than $20K annually are less likely to agree with first statement. Canadians aged 45-54 years are more likely to agree.

➤ Quebecers are more likely to agree with second statement. Younger Canadians (16-24 years) are less likely to agree.

➤ Younger Canadians (16-24) are less likely to agree with third statement. Older Canadians (55 plus years) are more likely to agree.

➤ Older Canadians (55 plus years) and those with high-school or less education are more likely to agree with the fourth statement. Those earning $70K or more annually and those with university education are less likely to agree.

➤ Younger Canadians (16-24 years) and those with university education are less likely to agree with fifth statement. Older Canadians (55 plus years) are more likely to agree.

Q.   Next I am going to read you a number of statements. Please rate the degree to which you agree or disagree with these statements using a 7-point scale, where 1 means you strongly disagree, 7 means you strongly agree and the midpoint 4 means you neither agree nor disagree.
Source: Ekos Research Associates, Rethinking Government '94.

Table 125 — *Self-Reliance*

	March-August 1987	
	General public %	Elites %
Agree	79	79
Disagree	20	19

Q.   Too many people want someone else to help them solve their problems instead of solving them themselves. Do you basically agree or basically disagree with that statement?
Source: Institute for Social Research, Attitudes toward Civil Liberties and the Canadian Charter of Rights.

Table 126 — Overall Perceptions

	February 1994 Mean (1 to 7)
All in all, government is a positive force in my life.	3.79
I don't really expect as much of government today as I did 10 years ago.	4.49

➤ No regional variances for first statement. Younger Canadians (25-34) less likely to agree with this statement. Older Canadians (55 plus years) are more likely to agree.

➤ No regional variances for second statement. Younger Canadians are more likely to agree.

Q. Next I am going to read you a number of statements. Please rate the degree to which you agree or disagree with these statements using a 7-point scale, where 1 means you strongly disagree, 7 means you strongly agree and the midpoint 4 means you neither agree nor disagree.
Source: Ekos Research Associates, Rethinking Government '94.

Table 127 — Perceptions of Waste in Government

	1988 %	1993 %
Waste a lot of the money we pay in taxes	64	80
Waste some of it	32	19
Don't waste very much of it	1	1

➤ Those with less education are most likely to agree that government is wasteful.

➤ Quebecers are most likely and Atlantic Canadians least likely to describe government as wasteful.

Q. Do you think that people in the government:
Source: Carleton University/Institute for Social Research, Canadian National Election Studies.

Table 128 — Views on Bureaucratic Inefficiency

	February 1994
	%
Agree	84
Neither agree nor disagree	9
Disagree	6
Mean (1 to 7)	5.94

Q. The real problem with the federal government is the waste and inefficiency of the bureaucracy.
Source: Ekos Research Associates, Rethinking Government '94.

Table 129 — Perceptions of Waste

	July 1988		
	Federal	Provincial	Municipal
	%	%	%
$0.0	1	2	4
$0.01 to $0.10	9	11	23
$0.11 to $0.25	22	27	24
$0.26 to $0.50	37	33	21
$0.50 to $0.75	6	7	4
$0.76 to $1.00	5	3	2
Don't know	19	19	21

Q. Out of every tax dollar that goes to the federal government in Ottawa, how many cents of each dollar would you say are wasted?
Q. And out of every tax dollar that goes to the government of this province, how many cents of each dollar would you say are wasted?
Q. And out of every tax dollar that goes to your local government, how many cents of each dollar would you say are wasted?
Source: Gallup Canada, The Gallup Poll.

Table 130 — Views on Social Security Reform and Waste

	June 1994 %
To make our social programs more effective and efficient all we need to do is clean up the waste and abuse.	44
Simply cleaning up waste and abuse is not enough – our social programs need to be completely overhauled.	54

➤ B.C. residents are less likely to state first statement closer to their point of view. Quebecers are more likely to state that it is closer to their point of view.

➤ Those with annual incomes of $60K or more were more likely to indicate that second statement was closer to their point of view. Quebecers were less likely to state that this statement was closest to their point of view.

Q. Which statement is closest to your own point of view?
Source: Angus Reid Group, Social Security Reform Wave II for Human Resources Development Canada.

Table 131 — Views on Efficiency in Health Care

	Spring 1994 %
Agree	84
Disagree	14

Q. Do you agree or disagree that cuts to medical services in Canada could be completely avoided if the health care system were just made more efficient?
Source: Insight Canada, Perspectives Canada.

Table 132 — Views on Waste in Health Care

	1989	1992	1994
		% agreeing	
Doctors often prescribe unnecessarily	64	70	72
Many people use health services they do not need	74	84	84
Many people in hospital could be looked after equally well at home	39	54	71
Hospitals do not manage their finances economically	63	69	55

➤ Men, older Canadians, and those with higher incomes are more likely to agree with misuse statements.

➤ However, seniors are less likely than other Canadians to agree that physicians prescribe unnecessarily, or that hospitals do not manage finances economically.

Q. *Thinking about health care costs, do you strongly agree, somewhat agree, somewhat disagree or strongly disagree with each of the following statements?*
Source: Price Waterhouse, The Canada Health Monitor.

Table 133 — Perceived Effectiveness of Federal Policy Re. "The Needy"

	Poor job %	Good job %
Summer 1988	50	40
Fall 1988	45	43
Summer 1989	58	32
Fall 1990	58	32
Historic average	53	37

➤ Atlantic Canadians, women, lower income quintiles, seniors and younger adults more likely to say federal government has done a "poor job."

Q. *Federal government's job in helping the needy (exact wording of question not available).*
Source: Decima Research: Decima Quarterly.

Table 134 — Trust in Institutions

	1993	
	% saying "a great deal"	% saying "none at all"
Armed forces	13	5
Organized religion	11	16
Education system	8	7
TV news	7	7
Legal system	5	11
Big business	4	13
Social security system	4	9
Newspapers	3	10
Federal government	3	16
Provincial government	3	23
Civil service	2	14

➤ Seniors are more likely to express confidence in the federal and provincial governments. Younger Canadians express greater confidence in big business than other Canadians.

➤ Those with less education are less likely to express confidence in the legal system, but more likely to express confidence in the police and in the military.

➤ British Columbians and Ontarians are least likely to express confidence in their provincial governments, and British Columbians are also least likely to express confidence in the federal government.

Q. *For each of the following institutions, please tell us how much confidence you have in them, a great deal, quite a lot, not very much or none at all?*
Source: *Carleton University/Institute for Social Research, Canadian National Election Studies.*

Table 135 — Belief in Government

	March-August 1987	
	General public %	Elites %
Threatens the rights of people and must not be trusted	11	6
Neither	22	22
Is the best instrument for promoting the general interests of society	56	68

➤ Older Canadians are more likely to say government promotes general interests.

➤ Ontarians are more likely to say government promotes general interests, while Quebecers are least likely.

Q. *Government by its nature:*
Source: *Institute for Social Research, Attitudes toward Civil Liberties and the Canadian Charter of Rights.*

Table 136 — Trust in Government

February 1994
Mean (1 to 7)

What really bothers me is that our politicians and business leaders
seem to have taken care of themselves and their friends while average
Canadians have suffered badly.   5.89

I think the ethical standards of our federal government have slipped
badly in the past decade.   5.33

I have lost all confidence in our current system of government.   4.31

➤ There are no regional or other demographic variances for the first statement.
➤ Quebecers and younger Canadians (16-24 years) are less likely to agree with the second statement. Older Canadians (55 plus years) are more likely to agree.
➤ Those with university education are less likely to agree with third statement. Quebecers are more likely to agree.

Q. *Now I am going to read you some more statements. Please rate the degree to which you agree or disagree with these statements using a 7-point scale where 1 means you strongly disagree, 7 means you strongly agree and the midpoint 4 means you neither agree nor disagree.*
Source: Ekos Research Associates, Rethinking Government '94.

Table 137 — Trust in Government

	1988 %	1993 %
Quite a few of the people running the government are a little crooked	46	46
Not very many are crooked	32	36
Hardly any of them are crooked	11	10

➤ Those with less education are more likely to express distrust, as are younger Canadians.

➤ Those earning in the mid-range ($20K to $59K) are more likely to express distrust.

Q. *Do you think that:*
Source: Carleton University/Institute for Social Research, Canadian National Election Studies.

Table 138 — Trust in Politicians

March-August 1987

	You can't trust politicians to tell the truth		Most politicians can be trusted to do what's best for the country.	
	General public %	Elites %	General public %	Elites %
Mostly true	63	43	53	65
Mostly false	24	50	33	29

➤ Quebecers are somewhat more distrustful, as are those of lower SES and younger Canadians.

Source: *Institute for Social Research*, Attitudes toward Civil Liberties and the Canadian Charter of Rights.

Table 139 — Trust in Government

	1988 %	1993 %
Just about always	3	2
Most of the time	45	32
Only some of the time	47	63

➤ Younger Canadians are more likely to express distrust.

➤ Atlantic Canadians and Ontarians are most trustful.

Q. How much of the time do you think you can trust the government in Ottawa to do what is right?
Source: *Carleton University/Institute for Social Research*, Canadian National Election Studies.

Table 140 — Trust in Reform Process

	June 1994 %
Strongly agree	11
Agree	23
Neutral	19
Disagree	25
Strongly disagree	22

➤ Albertans were less likely to agree with this statement, while those with annual incomes of less than $20K were more likely to agree.

Q.   I trust the federal government to make the changes that are necessary to reform our social programs.
Source: Angus Reid Group, Social Security Reform Wave II for Human Resources Development Canada.

Table 141 — Trust in Parties, Politicians and Bureaucracy

	1993 % agreeing	% disagreeing
Generally, those elected to Parliament soon lose touch with the people.	83	15
I don't think the government cares much what people like me think.	74	24
I'd rather put my trust in the down-to-earth thinking of ordinary people than in experts.	60	34
Political parties spend too much time catering to minorities.	55	37
All federal parties are basically the same; there isn't really a choice.	48	48

➤ Quebecers are less likely to agree that political parties spend too much time catering to minorities.
➤ Those with less education are more likely to express distrust of government.

Q.   In this section, we are interested in your views about how government works. For each statement below, please indicate if you strongly agree, agree, disagree, or strongly disagree by writing the number that best represents how you feel in the space at the right of each statement.
Source: Carleton University/Institute for Social Research, Canadian National Election Studies.

Table 142 — Attitudes Toward Electoral Process

	1993 %
Much better	1
Better	3
About the same	16
Worse	35
Much worse	36
Undecided	9

➤ The university educated are the most likely to say life would be worse.

Q.   *If we stopped having elections, do you think that life would be:*
Source: *Carleton University/Institute for Social Research*, Canadian National Election Studies.

Table 143 — Views on Citizen Participation

	1993 % agreeing	% disagreeing
In a democracy, no political decisions should be made in secret.	85	13
Most people have enough sense to tell whether the government is doing a good job.	72	27
We could probably solve most of our big national problems if decisions could be brought back to the people at the grass roots.	65	29
The problem with democracy is that most people don't really know what's best for them.	47	49
The government should pay the most attention to those citizens who are well informed.	46	49

➤ Older Canadians are more likely to agree that most people have the sense to tell if government is doing a good job and that government should pay the most attention to the well-informed.
➤ Those with less education are more likely to agree with all statements.
➤ Atlantic Canadians are most likely and British Columbians least likely to agree that most people don't know what's best for them.

Q.   *In this section, we are interested in your views about how government works. For each statement below, please indicate if you strongly agree, agree, disagree, or strongly disagree by writing the number that best represents how you feel in the space at the right of each statement.*
Source: *Carleton University/Institute for Social Research*, Canadian National Election Studies.

Table 144 — *Democratic versus Authoritarian Views of Government*

	March-August 1987	
	General public %	Elites %
Mainly agree	47	36
Mainly disagree	46	60

➤ Quebecers are least likely to agree.

Q.   *It will always be necessary to have a few strong, able people actually running everything.*
Source: *Institute for Social Research*, Attitudes toward Civil Liberties and the Canadian Charter of Rights.

Table 145 — *Views on Citizen Consultation*

	February/July 1994 Mean (1 to 7)
The Government of Canada must place much more emphasis on consulting its citizens.	5.84
I get the feeling that governments have lost sight of the needs of average Canadians.	5.59
I believe individual citizens like myself have to shoulder some of the blame for problems facing the country.	4.58
When the government consults with citizens, citizen views have real impact on government actions.	3.77

➤ No regional or other demographic variances for first statement.

➤ Younger Canadians (16-24 years) are less likely to agree with second statement.

➤ Quebecers are more likely to agree with third statement.

➤ Older Canadians (55 plus years) are more likely to agree with fourth statement.

Q.   *Now I'm going to read you a few statements. Please tell me how much you agree or disagree with each of them. Please use a 7-point scale where 1 is strongly disagree, 7 is strongly agree and the midpoint 4 is neither agree nor disagree.*
Source: *Ekos Research Associates*, Rethinking Government '94.

Table 146 — Preference for Consultation Method

	General public Mean (1 TO 7)	Elites Mean (1 to 7)
National elections	5.20	5.49
Referendum	4.69	4.17
Town hall meetings	4.56	3.92
Communication with individual MPs	4.50	4.09
Surveys/polls/focus groups	4.38	4.15
Public hearings by government bodies	4.24	—
Through special interest groups/ industry associations*	4.10	3.41
Royal commissions	3.60	3.04
Communication with public servants	—	3.71
Industry associations	—	4.31

Q. *There are a number of ways the federal government can consult the public. Please rate each of the following ways on a 7-point scale where 1 is not at all useful, 7 is extremely useful, and the midpoint 4 is moderately useful.*
* Elites were asked about "non-governmental organizations or interest groups" and "industry associations" separately.
Source: Ekos Research Associates, Rethinking Government '94.

Table 147 — Support for Social Programs

	1994			
	% saying "Strongly support"	% saying "Support"	% saying "Approve"	% saying "Strongly oppose"
Benefits for the disabled	59	34	1	1
Benefits for seniors	57	23	4	1
Programs to help young people get a job after finishing school	41	37	9	3
Unemployment insurance	35	37	10	4
Financial assistance for students attending university or college	34	38	12	3
Benefits for middle and low income families with children under 18 years of age living at home	32	40	10	2
Workers' compensation	31	40	12	3
Helping people who are employed upgrade their job skills	27	35	16	8
Welfare	18	32	21	9
Providing financial assistance to those who want to relocate to find a job	14	30	24	13

Q.   *I'm now going to ask you to tell me if you support or oppose the government continuing to provide specific social programs. You can express your opinion on each program by using a scale of 1 to 7 where "1" means you strongly oppose the government continuing to provide this program and "7" means you strongly support the government continuing to provide this specific program.*
Source: Angus Reid Group, Research conducted on behalf of Human Resources Development, 1994.